How to access the supplemental web resource

We are pleased to provide access to a web resource that supplements your textbook, *Beginning Hip-Hop Dance.* This resource offers video clips of hip-hop dance techniques, learning activities, assignments, interactive quizzes, and more.

Accessing the web resource is easy!
Follow these steps if you purchased a new book:

1. Visit **www.HumanKinetics.com/BeginningHipHopDance**.

2. Click the <u>first edition</u> link next to the book cover.

3. Click the Sign In link on the left or top of the page. If you do not have an account with Human Kinetics, you will be prompted to create one.

4. If the online product you purchased does not appear in the Ancillary Items box on the left of the page, click the Enter Key Code option in that box. Enter the key code that is printed at the right, including all hyphens. Click the Submit button to unlock your online product.

5. After you have entered your key code the first time, you will never have to enter it again to access this product. Once unlocked, a link to your product will permanently appear in the menu on the left. For future visits, all you need to do is sign in to the textbook's website and follow the link that appears in the left menu!

→ Click the Need Help? button on the textbook's website if you need assistance along the way.

How to access the web resource if you purchased a used book:

You may purchase access to the web resource by visiting the text's website, **www.HumanKinetics.com/BeginningHipHopDance**, or by calling the following:

800-747-4457 . . . . U.S. customers
800-465-7301 . . . . Canadian customers
+44 (0) 113 255 5665 . . . . European customers
217-351-5076 . . . . International customers

For technical support, send an e-mail to:
support@hkusa.com . . . . U.S. and international customers
info@hkcanada.com . . . . Canadian customers
academic@hkeurope.com . . . . European customers

HUMAN KINETICS

05-2018

This unique code allows you access to the web resource.

Access is provided if you have purchased a new book. Once submitted, the code may not be entered for any other user.

Product: Beginning Hip-Hop Dance web resource

Key code: DURDEN-A9RT4Q-OSG

D0140727

Beginning

HIP-HOP DANCE

INTERACTIVE DANCE SERIES

E. Moncell Durden

University of Southern California

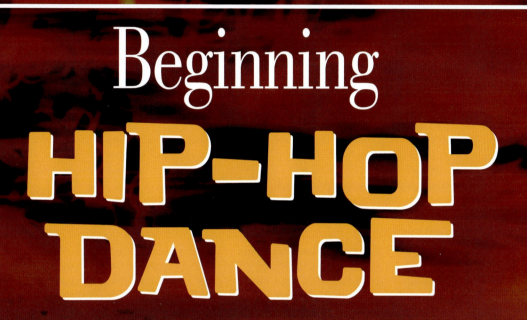

Human Kinetics

JESSAMINE COUNTY PUBLIC LIBRARY
600 South Main Street
Nicholasville, KY 40356
(859)885-3523

Library of Congress Cataloging-in-Publication Data

Names: Durden, E. Moncell.
Title: Beginning hip-hop dance / E. Moncell Durden, University of Southern California.
Description: Champaign, IL : Human Kinetics, [2019] | Series: Interactive dance series | Includes bibliographical references and index. |
Identifiers: LCCN 2018003363 (print) | LCCN 2018005443 (ebook) | ISBN 9781492544463 (e-book) | ISBN 9781492544456 (print)
Subjects: LCSH: Hip-hop dance.
Classification: LCC GV1796.H57 (ebook) | LCC GV1796.H57 D87 2019 (print) | DDC 793.3--dc23
LC record available at https://lccn.loc.gov/2018003363

ISBN: 978-1-4925-4445-6 (print)

Copyright © 2019 by Human Kinetics, Inc.

All rights reserved. Except for use in a review, the reproduction or utilization of this work in any form or by any electronic, mechanical, or other means, now known or hereafter invented, including xerography, photocopying, and recording, and in any information storage and retrieval system, is forbidden without the written permission of the publisher.

The web addresses cited in this text were current as of February 2018, unless otherwise noted.

Acquisitions Editor: Gayle Kassing, PhD; **Senior Developmental Editor:** Bethany J. Bentley; **Senior Managing Editor:** Amy Stahl; **Managing Editor:** Anna Lan Seaman; **Copyeditor:** Tom Tiller; **Indexer:** Bobbi Swanson; **Permissions Manager:** Dalene Reeder; **Senior Graphic Designer:** Joe Buck; **Graphic Designer:** Denise Lowry; **Cover Designer:** Keri Evans; **Cover Design Associate:** Susan Rothermel Allen; **Photograph (cover and interior):** Michael Yates/© Human Kinetics, unless otherwise noted; **Photo Asset Manager:** Laura Fitch; **Visual Production Assistant:** Joyce Brumfield; **Photo Production Manager:** Jason Allen; **Senior Art Manager:** Kelly Hendren; **Illustrations:** © Human Kinetics; **Printer:** Versa Press

We thank the Glorya Kaufman School of Dance at the University of Southern California in Los Angeles for assistance in providing the location for the photo and video shoot.

The video contents of this product are licensed for educational public performance for viewing by a traditional (live) audience, via closed circuit television, or via computerized local area networks within a single building or geographically unified campus. To request a license to broadcast these contents to a wider audience—for example, throughout a school district or state, or on a television station—please contact your sales representative (**www.HumanKinetics.com/SalesRepresentatives**).

Printed in the United States of America   10 9 8 7 6 5 4 3 2 1

The paper in this book is certified under a sustainable forestry program.

Human Kinetics
P.O. Box 5076
Champaign, IL 61825-5076
Website: www.HumanKinetics.com

In the United States, email info@hkusa.com or call 800-747-4457.
In Canada, email info@hkcanada.com.
In the United Kingdom/Europe, email hk@hkeurope.com.

For information about Human Kinetics' coverage in other areas of the world, please visit our website: **www.HumanKinetics.com**

E6942

CONTENTS

Preface   v
How to Use the Web Resource   vii
Acknowledgments   viii

1 Introduction to Hip-Hop Dance   1

Defining Hip-Hop Dance 2
Benefits of Studying Hip-Hop Dance 3
Basics of Hip-Hop Dance 3
Expectations and Etiquette for Students 6
Evaluation of Your Class Performance 7
Structure of the Hip-Hop Class 8
Summary 11

2 Preparing for Class   13

Dressing for Class 13
Carrying Dance Gear 15
Preparing Yourself Mentally and Physically 16
Summary 18

3 Safety and Health   19

Studio Safety 20
Personal Safety 21
Basic Anatomy 22
Basic Kinesiology 25
Preventing Common Dance Injuries 27
Treating Common Dance Injuries 29
Warming Up 30
Understanding Fitness 31
Nutrition, Hydration, and Rest 32
Summary 33

4 Basics of Hip-Hop Technique 35

BEATS Approach. 36
Alignment and Stance 39
Isolation Grooves 40
Across the Floor 48
Performance Directions. 49
Summary 49

5 Basic Hip-Hop Dance Steps 51

Dances From the 1980s 52
Dances From the 1990s 61
Dances From the Early 2000s 66
Summary 71

6 History of Hip-Hop Dance 73

Origins of Hip-Hop Dance 73
Appropriation and Approximation of Hip-Hop 82
Commercialization of Hip-Hop Dance 84
Summary 86

7 Hip-Hop Dance Forms 87

Locking 88
Waacking 91
Electric Boogaloos and Popping 93
House 97
Summary 99

Glossary 101
References 105
Index 107
About the Author 111

PREFACE

I define the term *dance* acronymically as "Discovering the Autobiographical self by Negotiating Creativity and Expression." More specifically, we are in constant discovery of our autobiographical self, our narrative, and we are negotiating our bodies, ideals, voice, expression space, emotions, and so on; our creativity is the production of the feelings, and expression is the space in which we allow ourselves to be vulnerable to share those feelings with others. Hip-hop dance is an ever-changing multicultural expression of individuality, innovation, and communication. Even though hip-hop is an ever-growing movement, hip-hop culture still consists of basic elements: rapping, deejaying, graffiti art, beatboxing, and the dance forms of b-boying (breaking) and hip-hop social dances.

Beginning Hip-Hop Dance takes you on a personal journey into the essence of hip-hop and its dance forms. The book gives you a platform on which to build a working knowledge of hip-hop dance by participating in hip-hop exercises; learning movement vocabulary and dance technique; and developing hip-hop literacy by exploring its history, lineage, and dance forms.

The book's chapter divisions offer structure for what can seem to be an improvisational dance genre. Chapter 1 briefly overviews hip-hop dance and examines what to expect in a hip-hop dance class. Chapter 2 addresses how to prepare for class both mentally and physically, including the best footwear choices for this style of dance and the proper clothing to wear during class. Chapter 3 covers personal and studio safety, basic anatomy and kinesiology, nutrition and hydration, and injury prevention and treatment.

Chapter 4 shifts the focus to the dancing itself by addressing the basics of hip-hop dance; it also explains the BEATS method (which focuses on body, emotion, action, time, and space) for learning hip-hop. Chapter 5 follows up by introducing you to basic hip-hop dances. Chapter 6 explores the development and lineage of hip-hop dance; along the way, it highlights cultural phenomena that help construct and characterize hip-hop movement practices, as well as their aesthetic values. Finally, chapter 7 gives you insight into six major forms of hip-hop dance: locking, waacking, breaking or b-boying, popping and boogaloo, hip-hop, and house.

Beginning Hip-Hop Dance intertwines the visual, auditory, and kinesthetic modes of learning. It guides you along your hip-hop journey and gives you a platform for beginning to investigate your own ideals; it also enables you to develop the technique and knowledge to build on the movements presented here. You can find more information about technique, as well as video clips of each hip-hop movement presented in the book, in the online web resource. This web resource will be your companion during your journey of self-discovery through hip-hop dance. It includes chapter-by-chapter learning experiences, quizzes, and glossary terms, which are presented both with and without their definitions so that you can self-test your knowledge.

Thus *Beginning Hip-Hop Dance* gives you the tools you need in order to get started in the exciting and fulfilling world of hip-hop dance. However, in order to fully understand and develop the nuances, self-confidence, and attitudes that characterize this dance form, you must also take part in relevant social interactions, which can be found in club settings, at dance jams, and at practice jam sessions. Remember, this is *your* journey of self-discovery through hip-hop dance. Learning any new dance genre or form requires patience, so take your time, indulge in the information presented here, and find your own dance expression. Congratulations on taking your first steps!

HOW TO USE THE WEB RESOURCE

In a hip-hop dance class, steps and combinations can occur quickly. They can contain a large number of new movements or small additions to movements you have already learned. But you have an added advantage! Your personal tutor is just a few clicks away and is always available to help you remember and practice the exercises and steps executed in class. You can study between class meetings or when doing mental practice to memorize exercises or movement. Check out the web resource that accompanies the book online.

The web resource is an interactive tool that you can use to enhance your understanding of beginning hip-hop dance technique, review what you studied in class, or prepare for performance testing. It includes information about selected positions or movements, including instructions for correct performance; and video clips of hip-hop dance techniques. Also included are interactive quizzes for each chapter of the *Beginning Hip-Hop Dance* text, which let you test your knowledge of concepts, hip-hop dance basics, terminology, and more.

In a beginning hip-hop dance class, students learn about hip-hop technique, hip-hop dance as an art form, and themselves. The Supplementary Materials section of the web resource contains the following additional components for each chapter of the *Beginning Hip-Hop Dance* text. These components support both learning in the hip-hop dance class and exploring more about the world of hip-hop dance.

- Glossary terms from the text are presented so that you can check your knowledge of the translated meaning of the term as well as a description of the term.
- Web links give you a starting place to learn more about hip-hop dance techniques or styles.
- Chapters include e-journaling prompts that will help you think more deeply about beginning hip-hop dance class.
- Other assignments include specific activities to apply concepts and ideas about hip-hop dance.

This web resource helps you individualize your learning experience so that you can connect to, expand, and apply your learning of beginning hip-hop dance, enhancing your success and enjoyment in the study of this dance form.

ACKNOWLEDGMENTS

This book is dedicated to the hip hop dance community worldwide. Special acknowledgment goes to Rebecca A. White, Raymond G. White, Mary E. Brooks, E. Moncell Durden Jr., Tony "Ynot" Denaro, and Celine Kiner.

Chapter 1

Introduction to Hip-Hop Dance

Now one of the most popular forms of dance in the world, hip-hop arose in the Bronx in the early 1970s in the form of **b-boying**. It began to attract mainstream attention from both American and global audiences when it was featured in the 1983 film *Flashdance* (Simpson, Bruckheimer, & Lyne, 1983). In particular, one scene that focused on **breaking** inspired young people around the world to investigate this dance form. The solo dances (also referred to as social or party dances) of the 1980s continued to gain global popularity through rap concerts and music videos featured on the television series *Yo! MTV Raps*. Breaking was the first dance to represent the emerging cultural expression of hip-hop, those elements included but not limited to the following elements:

- Graffiti art, the visual language of the hip-hop community
- Deejaying, which represents the sounds and memories of the community
- Beatboxing, a form of vocal percussion that primarily mimics a beatbox drum machine
- Emceeing, which involves the voices and storytellers of the community

- B-boying, a form of "street" dance that originated with Puerto Rican and African American youth in the early 1970s and has been defined by one dance historian as "physical graffiti" (Banes, 1981)

As the dance form that accompanied this new culture, breaking was performed primarily to the **break** section of any record with a funky beat. This new and unique dance form required particular skills that not everyone had—or was even physically capable of developing. In the mid-1980s, however, the rise of hip-hop music led to a new movement including party dances that could be easily enjoyed by everyone. These new dances became known simply as *hip-hop* because that was the style of music to which they were performed.

DEFINING HIP-HOP DANCE

Hip-hop is characterized by a high level of playfulness and exploration through "move-meant" concepts and techniques—that is, moves that hold meaning and value, informed by personal, social, cultural, and environmental experiences. Hip-hop social dances feature multiple rhythms, as well as movement that generates and expands from multiple centers; in other words, it is **polyrhythmic** and **polycentric**.

Hip-hop dance does *not* use movement practices from modern, ballet, or Broadway- or Hollywood-style jazz dance. Rather, like African, authentic jazz, and other **African-diasporic** dance forms (such as Afro-Cuban, Brazilian, and Haitian), hip-hop employs a curved spine, bent knees, and an orientation to the earth. It is percussive, improvisational, and communal—for example, using call-and-response. It also uses pantomime and **isolations**, and it deeply engages the full body—neck, shoulders, arms, torso, rear end, hips, legs, knees, and feet. It is fluid, and the feet are flexed, not pointed.

The technique and structure of hip-hop are rooted in cultural concepts and traditions associated with behavioral characteristics of African dance heritage. New hip-hop dances are created all the time, and some recent popular forms include the Milly Rock, the Dab, Hit Dem Folks, the Drop, the Nae Nae, and the Whip, just to name a few. These dances engage and communicate African American cultural values such as the exhibition of cool, ideals of style, use of multiple rhythms, musical and spatial awareness, gesturing, attitude, fashion, spirituality, and individuality. These dance practices do not simply retain African American values; they enact philosophical theories as people place ancestral roots in new soil.

Black vernacular dance practices are usually defined by the music to which they are danced; thus jazz dance goes with jazz music, house dance with house music, and hip-hop dance with hip-hop music. More specifically, hip-hop dance is defined by two forms: b-boying, which is danced to breaks or breakbeat music, and hip-hop social dances, which are danced to rap music.

The use of a break in songs originated in soul music and involves sampling or repetition of an instrumental section. A break is usually characterized by all elements dropping out except for the drummer, and it can be established at the beginning, middle, or end of a record. For example, in the James Brown song "Funky Drummer," the break occurs at 5:22. A break can also come from any style of music. For instance, the first 18 seconds of the Beatles' "Sgt. Pepper's Lonely Hearts Club Band" constitute a break, as do the first four bars of Aerosmith's "Walk This Way." Perhaps the most concise definition of a break was offered by Afrika Bambaataa, who is considered the godfather of hip-hop: The break "is the part of the record everyone waits to dance to" (personal communication, 2007).

In the beginning of hip-hop, emcees and deejays used music samples from soul, funk, electronic, and rock records. Emcees would rhyme over the break, and breakers and solo dancers would dance. However, the commercialization and exploitation of breaking in the mid-1980s—along with the growing production of danceable rap records—led to a shift away from breaking and toward a new style of hip-hop dance. This new style included many solo dances, such as Happy Feet, the Roger Rabbit, the Biz Markie, the Running Man, and the Skate. (These steps and more are described in chapter 5.)

BENEFITS OF STUDYING HIP-HOP DANCE

Hip-hop dance helps you identify and explore your individual characteristics, your personal preferences, and your own style; it also provides a physical outlet for your emotions. Hip-hop is not, however, only about performance and presentation. It also involves communication, collaboration, community building, critical and creative thinking, innovation, and problem solving. In addition, it builds stronger motor skills, focus, memory, coordination, and fitness. In other words, it gives you a way to illuminate personal and cultural dynamics of ethnicity and diversity while also providing you with a vast and powerful repertoire for self-expression.

BASICS OF HIP-HOP DANCE

Dance can be used to express ideas through gesticulations that correspond visually with certain concepts. In hip-hop, those concepts begin with three key ingredients: the music, the environment, and you. The relationships between the music, your sociocultural experience, and your body in motion exist in a type of nonverbal conversation about feelings that are in conversation with each other at the same time.

Music is the guide; it tells you when to start, jump, turn, **drop**, spin, and stop. Movement ideas, however, can come from anywhere—for example, from games that children play, the ways in which your friends walk or gesture when they talk with each other, moves used by people playing basketball in the park, or movements exhibited by skateboarders. In hip-hop dance, these movements and movement concepts are reconfigured and presented in various forms, such as **bouncing**, **rocking**, **grooving**, isolations, polyrhythms, polycentrism, pausing, improvisation, and innovation. These movements and concepts are not indigenous to hip-hop but date back hundreds of years. The expression is based on one's current life experience, but many of the gestures are connected to and relate back to nonverbal communication practices that exist in one's community or culture. It is like the saying, "There is nothing new under the sun," but what is new is you; you bring new expressive approaches.

Dance Environment

Your dance class may take place in a dedicated dance space or in a room that serves many purposes. It may occur, for instance, in a fairly large room with metal or wooden railings, called *barres*, that help ballet students maintain their balance during certain exercises. Dance studios also tend to have wooden or vinyl floors with "sprung" flooring underneath that gives when you jump or land. In addition, the room may have mirrors lining one wall in order to help your instructor see everyone in the room and to help both you and your instructor see your form and **alignment**. Although mirrors may seem intimidating at first, you will quickly become accustomed to using them as a way to learn.

In contrast, some dance classes take place in a gym or auditorium with no barres or mirrors. A lack of mirrors is not necessarily a bad thing in hip-hop dance. Although hip-hop does feature some specific head, arm, leg, and foot positions, it ultimately focuses more on how you *feel* than on how you look when dancing. Therefore, the use of a mirror can be an inhibiting factor as the teacher works to encourage you to build and rely on your own **kinesthetic awareness**. In this approach, you learn to know by feeling rather than by seeing.

Moreover, social dances such as hip-hop are born out of a specific community's sociocultural concepts of nonverbal communication. As a result, these dances are not always learned in a studio. Instead, they can be learned in public spaces and events in the community (such as dance halls, social clubs, house parties, and playgrounds) and other nonstudio practice locations (such as sidewalks, shopping malls, and train and subway stations; any place a dancer feels like practicing). These dances constitute forms of expression that hold particular value in their community. Therefore, learning social hip-hop dances requires more than developing technical acuity; it also involves learning the who, what, when, where, why, and how of a cultural practice. The dances are inspired by the music, the music comes from the people, and the thought processes of the people are informed by their sociocultural experiences.

Role of the Teacher

Your teacher is your personal guide to the music, movement, language, history, and culture of hip-hop. He or she imparts knowledge through systematic methods to help you draw out or develop your own dancing.

Every dance teacher is different, and each brings his or her own perspective to the class. Some teachers take a choreographic approach, in which you learn a routine to a specific song or section of a song. This type of class is sometimes referred to as **commercial** hip-hop or *choreo*. Other teachers take a more **fundamental** approach, which teaches students key technical aspects of hip-hop, such as how to groove. These teachers then help students strengthen their improvisation skills through learning current popular dances, as well as popular ones from the 1980s and 1990s (for example, the Bart Simpson and the Harlem Shake). Still others may have a personal idea of what hip-hop movement means to them. As a student, then, you have to know what you're looking for—what is important to you—and find a teacher who provides that quality, knowledge, and inspiration.

At the same time, whatever approach a teacher uses (traditional, foundational, or current social hip-hop), he or she must share one common aspect of teaching hip-hop dance—namely, a working knowledge of the dance form, its vocabulary, its techniques, and its history. For instance, the teacher must know what it means to dance in a **cypher**, which takes the shape of (and is sometimes referred to as) a circle. This is where the dance conversation happens, as people gather and use rap or dance to display their skill. Here, dancers exhibit physical and emotional skill and share what they have to say through movement. Teachers must also know which music goes with which form of movement or dance, understand how to hold conversations with music through call-and-response, and possess a high level of improvisational skill.

In addition, teachers must robustly comprehend hip-hop's concepts of communication, which, as noted earlier, engage with African American values such as the exhibition of cool, the use of polyrhythm, and individuality. In this context, the teacher's role is to provide encouragement and guidance in order to help you build self-awareness and confidence. More specifically, your teacher can steer you in the right direction to identify safe and sequential conditioning techniques, daily health practices (such as exercise, rest, and a balanced diet), resources for research, and best practices for meeting and expanding your potential.

Role of the Student

As a student of hip-hop dance, you are called not only to appear in class but also to play an important role in it. Resolve to be an active and engaged participant; for starters, respect yourself, your teacher, your peers, and the practice environment. Maintain your intellectual curiosity. Refrain from making comparisons and judging yourself negatively based on what others are doing; that type of mentality distracts you from reaching your own full potential. Everyone picks movement up differently, and what may be easy for you could be difficult for someone else, or vice versa. Enjoy the process.

Remember that everyone is there because they want to learn. The class will give you a chance to learn not only about hip-hop dance but also about how you learn—that is, how things work for you. To make the most of this opportunity, bring an openness and a willingness to try new things. Allow yourself to be vulnerable enough to grow and take ownership of your mistakes. Your mistakes are simply things you didn't mean to do. That doesn't make them wrong; look at them as new possibilities.

In fact, there is always more to learn, and even a dancer with years

TECHNIQUE TIP

Don't compare yourself with other dancers in class. No single body type is best for hip-hop dance, other than a healthy one. Hip-hop is not about shaping yourself to a mold; it is about finding your artistic voice through dance.

of practice can benefit from more learning. If you are a beginner, jump into learning hip-hop dance with both feet. Have fun! Dance is a life practice, and you are forever a student, so leave behind any attitudes that hinder a positive learning environment. Replace negative sayings such as "I can't" with more self-empowering affirmations such as "I can" and "I will." Open yourself to your unlimited potential for achievement.

EXPECTATIONS AND ETIQUETTE FOR STUDENTS

Check yourself at the door and enter the space as a receptive vessel, ready to engage and explore. Leave problems, worries, and negative attitudes outside. Your personal and professional attitudes toward your classmates, the dance space, and your teacher represent the value and respect you give to them—and to yourself. Show up to class well prepared mentally, physically, and emotionally. Be ready to listen, observe, participate, share, encourage, and, above all, inspire and be inspired.

Listen to the instructions provided by your teacher, and listen to your classmates when they address the class. Don't listen only with your ears; listen with your whole body—your eyes, your body language, and your mind. Observe through active participation how the instructor is guiding you in an exercise. Participate by making an offering to the cypher, whether in the form of movement or verbalization, as well as by exploring your feelings and giving attention to others and to the space. Respect your teachers and classmates by listening attentively and waiting until the instructor asks for questions.

Preparing and Practicing

You are, of course, expected to come to each class wearing appropriate attire (see chapter 2). Preparation also includes practicing what you learned in the previous class session. The practice time provided during class is not enough for you to fully learn movements or steps. You must set aside some time every day to practice the new movements and combinations that you have learned.

To help you prepare for class, make mental notes or write down new steps for future practice; also take notes about what you liked most in each class session and build on those ideas for your personal growth. Outside of class, find practice partners and use all resources that your teacher provides. For example, most dance teachers are available after class or by appointment if you need extra instruction. In addition, take advantage of any extra practice or rehearsal times offered. Record your practices sessions on video, then watch them and take notes about areas in which you need or wish to improve.

Being Present and Prompt

Come to class consistently and show up on time. Missing a class puts you behind in skill development. Arriving late disrupts the flow of the class and may cause you to miss important warm-ups or reviews. In addition, either missing classes or arriving late may indicate that you do not take the class or the teacher seriously. If you must miss a class, contact your teacher regarding the skills you missed and find out how you can make up any practice times. Absences may justify grade reduction, if you are being graded, and too many absences could cause you to fail the course.

EVALUATION OF YOUR CLASS PERFORMANCE

Evaluation of your work in the class is based on the quality of your participation in class movement and discussion sessions, as well as any assignments. Your individual progress is evaluated in all content areas of the course, including the following:

- Knowledge of hip-hop forms, dance techniques, and other class material
- Ability to apply corrections
- Proper execution of set combinations
- Degree of improvement
- Class attendance and punctuality
- Consistency of participation in all class activities
- Conceptual clarity (clear intention of movement) and degree of involvement in any creative projects
- Thoughtfulness toward others and the learning environment

The Tone Wop.

STRUCTURE OF THE HIP-HOP CLASS

The structure of a hip-hop class may vary depending on the teacher and his or her personal philosophy. Most classes, however, include the following elements: warm-up, technique and groove, moving across the floor, and cool-down. The following description is just one example of how a beginner hip-hop class might be structured.

Warm-Up

Warming up does more than prepare your body physically for rigorous activity. It also prepares you mentally and emotionally by gradually arousing your cardiovascular system, thus increasing blood flow to your muscles. The heart pumps more blood as our heart rate increases; this prepares large muscles to be physically active. In addition, warm-up exercises prepare you to perform the foundational movements that allow you to best execute the dance form—for instance, joint mobilization isolations; articulation of the neck, spine, and hips; corporeal fluidity and timing; and moves such as drops, bouncing, rocking, weight changes, polyrhythms, and jumps. In other words, warm-up exercises prepare you specifically to use your body to perform the dance.

In order to achieve these goals, your warm-up time should be devoted mainly to developing proper posture while also strengthening your technique. In this way, the warm-up allows your body to figure out the basic movement mechanics needed in order to execute combinations and practice exercises. In some classes, the warm-up also includes light stretching to increase your flexibility and help prevent injury.

Technique and Groove

Your fluidity in executing hip-hop technique is determined by your ability to reach a high level of expressivity and visualization of rhythms between the music and the body. Hip-hop is grounded in the following techniques:

- Bounces are the foundational movements in all hip-hop social dances that involve leg movement.
- Polyrhythms move the body through multiple rhythms heard in the music.
- Polycentric movements are initiated from multiple centers.
- Isolations involve movement of one body part without relation to other body parts.
- Rocking involves gentle movement from front to back or from side to side; it can be done either with or without isolations.

These techniques may be presented in any order in a dance class, but it is most common to begin with bounces due to their foundational importance. The teacher may demonstrate these techniques, then show dances that use a particular technique for you to practice. Once you have practiced enough, the teacher may add hip-hop dance sequences that use a combination of techniques. Each dance will include consistent use of a staple movement, which could involve the legs, arms, neck, hips, booty, hands, torso, or some combination of these.

If, for example, a sequence uses a particular movement of the legs, the rest of the body responds through the creative facility of improvisation. Thus, even though your legs are doing the same movements as the legs of

DID YOU KNOW?

Bounces exist in all forms of dance, though they are not called *bounces* in other dance forms. For instance, you can find bounces in African dances, African-diasporic dance, minuets, and even ballet—each marked by its own style.

the person next to you, you demonstrate your individuality through your choice of timing, direction, levels (in terms of height and body position), and body parts. Your goal should be to execute these movement techniques with a strong sense of groove—that is, of moving smoothly with the tempo of the record or musicians.

Moving Across the Floor

In order to build on the warm-up and technique sections, the teacher will have you reuse those movements in combinations, or steps across the floor. Moving either as an individual or in a group, you can use everything from stylized walking to particular dances drawn from multiple generations, such as the Roger Rabbit, the Running Man, the BK Bounce, the Nae Nae, the Wu-Tang, and the Milly Rock. Moving across the floor in this way strengthens your technique and develops your endurance, sense of improvisation and rhythmic play, timing, weight distribution, groove, sensibility, spatial awareness, and musicality.

Improvising different movements.

These traveling steps may also help you in the creative process of determining how a dance will move across the floor. Thus, as the class progresses, your teacher may begin to combine the dance steps to create sequences of movement.

Floor Movements and Exercises

Your dance class may include floor movements if your teacher is showing you movements from b-boying or hip-hop ground movements. The movements addressed during this portion of class may involve dropping to the floor and getting back up in a steady and fluid movement, staying low to the ground, or sitting on the ground. These exercises require a great deal of balance, coordination, weight shifting, rhythmic timing, flexibility, core strength, and, sometimes, upper-body strength.

Ground movements apply multiple approaches, which may include attacking the floor, melting into the floor, or sliding along the floor, as well as rising or jumping from the floor and landing back on the floor. These approaches provide opportunities for improvisation and ownership in creating—and sometimes even naming—a movement that is specific to your body, even if it was initially inspired by someone or something else.

Movement Combinations and Sequences

In hip-hop, a movement combination pulls together individual dances or steps to create a phrase. The next stage is a **sequence**—a longer and more inclusive use of techniques and movements. A sequence can either work the total space of the studio, including the floor, or remain in the center. It may last anywhere from several counts of eight to the full length of a two- or three-minute song, in which case it becomes a **routine**, or longer choreographed sequence. How things play out depends on the teacher and the energy of the class. This is the part of the class where you apply what you have learned in terms of vocabulary, terminology, and technique.

While teaching a sequence, the teacher may split the class into smaller groups and have them either demonstrate one at a time, face each other while dancing at the same time, or engage in a dance battle. The teacher may also have you face a mirror while dancing, then turn you away from the mirror, in order to develop not only your coordination and motor skill but also your ability to explore how you feel. Sometimes the way you interpret a hip-hop ethos—or the way you experience the music—is more important than how you look while doing the movements. Developing strong technique is important, but you are an individual first. No one can feel the music in the same way you do or respond with your style, your narrative, and your approach. With this perspective in mind, play with the rhythm and timing of the sequence's steps and dances. Originality and individuality aren't just appreciated in hip-hop—they are expected (Malone, 1996).

After learning how to sequence, you learn how to create choreography, which is a more comprehensive sequence of movements. Choreography also involves spacing, **canons** (overlapping sequences), and, potentially, theatricality (miming).

Cool-Down

As with sport practices and other physically rigorous activities, the cool-down in dance is just as important as the warm-up. You can choose from multiple approaches to cooling down your body after a dance class. One way is to gradually slow down while using the movement from the sequence. Once you learn the sequence, you may run it a number of times so that everyone has enough time to explore the movement and work on developing their groove, flow, bounces, transitions, and steps. Then, rather than going from this high-intensity movement straight into stretching, your teacher may have you repeat the sequence or combination to a slower piece of music until your heart rate slows and you are ready to stretch.

During the beginning of the class, your teacher may have included light stretching as part of the warm-up. Even so, stretching at the end of class helps rejuvenate fatigued muscles. It also decreases the risk of injury, reduces soreness and spasms, reduces muscle tension, helps the body feel more relaxed, prevents joint strains, and aids circulation. Take care, however, not to overstretch, which can strain your muscles.

Do not stretch in any of the following conditions:

- You experienced a sprain or strain during class.
- Your range of motion is limited because of some type of injury.
- You have an inflamed joint.
- Your body is not warmed up.

To signify that class is finished, the teacher may use a certain movement to facilitate reflection on lessons learned—for example, a unified clap. This movement might also be initiated by students. As you leave class, it is courteous to thank the teacher.

SUMMARY

Hip-hop is both a form of dance and a means of communication that is informed by your everyday lived experience. It is not static; rather, it is always growing, and it speaks to changes in both music and society. It involves unique techniques, structure, vocabulary, aesthetics, and history. Hip-hop dance teaches you about musicality, polyrhythms and polycentrism, and isolations in a way that not many other dance forms can do. It is an empowering dance form in which individuality is not only appreciated but also expected and celebrated. Therefore, in hip-hop, the dancer is able to create and name steps and movements and build individual confidence while reinforcing community support.

To find supplementary materials for this chapter, such as learning activities, e-journal assignments, and web links, visit the web resource online.

Chapter 2

Preparing for Class

Learning a new art form is an exciting part of your education. Learning hip-hop dance in particular gives you an opportunity to express yourself in a new way and to explore a world of movement that is fun, interactive, and easy to learn. It is also one of the most popular dance forms in American culture. To help you make the most of that opportunity, this chapter discusses dressing properly for class, carrying your dance gear, and preparing yourself both mentally and physically. You can use this information to prepare yourself to be challenged, enlightened, exhilarated, and transformed during your hip-hop course.

DRESSING FOR CLASS

Dressing properly is crucial to making a good first impression. Proper attire suggests that you take seriously the dance form, the teacher, the class, and the learning environment. Specifically, wear comfortable, loose, nonrestrictive clothing in which you can move freely—for example, sweatpants, a t-shirt, or other dance apparel. Do not wear denim or other restrictive material. Nor should you come to class camera ready—that is, with heavy makeup, styled hair, or painted nails—unless the teacher asks you to do so.

In your hip-hop dance class, you will make full use of the studio floor. Therefore, kneepads may be helpful—not the bulky volleyball type but thinly padded protective knee braces that have "wings" or padding on the sides and in the back to fully protect the knee (see figure 2.1). You should also remove jewelry and watches for safety. In addition, if you have long hair, secure it so that it does not obstruct your view or the instructor's ability to see your face and does not cause a distraction or potential safety hazard due to the whipping effect when you move.

Figure 2.1 Thinly padded kneepad that works well for hip-hop dance practice.

SAFETY TIP

Over time, dancing with rubber-soled shoes on vinyl flooring will damage your ankles and knees; it may even cause knee dislocation because of the stickiness created between the shoe surface and the floor. Therefore, if you are dancing on vinyl flooring, try wearing socks over your sneakers to create a smoother interface.

Wear appropriate shoes, such as flat-bottomed sneakers or other shoes with large air-cushioning units in the heel to help absorb impact forces. Though it may seem counterintuitive, jazz shoes are *not* recommended, because they lack the cushioning and support required for hip-hop. Also, do not wear your street shoes in the dance studio. Designate another pair just for class in order to avoid tracking in dirt and debris. This approach shows respect for other dancers in your class, as well as those in other classes who use the same space and may dance barefoot.

CARRYING DANCE GEAR

Dancers typically carry a dance bag with them to hold their shoes and other items they will need either during or after class. You can find bags designed specifically for dance gear at dance apparel stores and online retailers, but gym bags also work well. Bags can become heavy when they contain a collection of stuff that you rarely need or use, so make wise choices about what to bring with you. Here are some items to consider:

- Sweat towel
- Deodorant
- Hair wraps, rubber bands, or bobby pins
- A separate or plastic bag for used clothing (especially if wet)
- Personal grooming items and extra towel if you plan to shower after class
- Water bottle and light snack for after class
- Separate pair of shoes for class

After class, although it is easy to simply drop your worn dance clothes and shoes into your dance bag, zip it up, and go, doing so is a bad habit. Instead, if your class occurs early in the day, or if the weather is warm, separate your damp practice clothes from your shoes and from other items in your bag. Then, as soon as you get home, remove the damp items, air out your shoes, and leave your dance bag open for a while before packing for your next class. Otherwise, mildew and germs can grow in the damp, dark space of the bag.

The Whip.

PREPARING YOURSELF MENTALLY AND PHYSICALLY

When rushing from one class or activity to the next, it can be easy to forget that personal preparation is vital to having a good class. To give yourself adequate time to prepare your mind and body for class, make a habit of arriving at the studio 10 to 15 minutes early. Personal warm-ups are most effective when they progress from mental to physical preparation.

Mental Preparation

If you have to transition immediately from sitting for an hour in an academic class to engaging in movement in a dance class, the process can be jarring to both your mind and your body. To ease the transition, take time to adjust your attitude and then visualize the work that lies ahead. This deliberateness can help you release tension, focus your mind, and make the most of your time in class.

Attitude

Attitude is a particular way of thinking or feeling about someone or something. It is reflected in a person's behavior, and a positive attitude can yield positive results. In other words, attitude determines altitude, in the sense of how high one can go (figuratively) in performing. Saying "I can't [do something]" is a form of psychological self-sabotage; indeed, saying it, can make it come true.

Dance is a nonverbal conversation. If you are open to new experiences and free from the fear of failing, then you can excel in helping your body speak. In order to become a strong dancer, you must allow yourself to be vulnerable enough to make mistakes. In fact, you must own your mistakes! A mistake is just something you didn't mean to do, which doesn't make it wrong. Therefore, you can take ownership of the "mistake" and develop it into something that becomes part of your **repertoire**. You can even turn a mistake into a signature movement or combination of your own.

Visualization

Dance involves developing not only your physical body but also your emotional, musical, and mental body. You have to work consistently from a place of mental power. To that end, **visualization** involves vividly imagining your success, both in dance class and in life. For example, as part of practices or rehearsals, you can visualize yourself going through the movements and choreography. See yourself performing a key move well and developing it more strongly. Exceptional dancers use visualization as part of their regular practice.

Self-Encouragement

The language of self-encouragement can play an important role in how much you believe in yourself. Positive words can help you reinforce a positive attitude, which, as discussed earlier, can lead to positive results. Words carry great power, and the meanings that you put into your words can either diminish or boost your self-confidence. You are the author of your story. Choose powerful words to describe yourself, your intention, your ability, your worth, and your potential.

At the same time, hip-hop calls you to think beyond yourself. It is about community building, and in this case your class is your community. Therefore, instead of thinking "I can" and "I will," think "we can" and "we will." Think and speak words of power to help you achieve your goals; the power of those words will manifest your reality and encourage your community.

> ## TECHNIQUE TIP
> Hip-hop dance is a whole-body activity. Therefore, inability to perform a given step does not necessarily result from a lack of strength. Instead, certain muscles may be affected by poor alignment, imbalance, lack of flexibility, or improper initiation of movement. Often, then, the solution is not only to increase the strength of individual muscles but also to consider your whole-body coordination. To enable your best effort, work to improve the key elements of strength, endurance, and flexibility.

Physical Preparation

Hip-hop is an active and highly athletic genre of dance, and its physical rigors demand a disciplined approach. As with any other aerobic activity, hip-hop dance can be physically taxing. Therefore, you must prepare your body with proper nutrition, hydration, and rest (see chapter 3).

Muscular Strength and Endurance

Muscular strength consists of a muscle's ability to exert maximal force against resistance, whereas **muscular endurance** consists of the muscle's ability to maintain the application of force over time. Hip-hop dance improves muscular endurance by forcing muscles to perform repeated contractions. This activity also improves muscle tone, tendon and ligament strength, bone density, balance, and stability—all of which improve overall physical capacity.

Flexibility

Flexibility consists of a joint's ability to move freely through the full range of motion. Good range of motion helps enable many of the exciting visual images that dancers are known for creating. The most common method for improving flexibility—and thus maximizing range of motion—is to engage in stretching. This practice should be included in a foundational hip-hop class to prepare dancers for more advanced technical work. As part of your pre-class routine, consider spending the second half of your personal warm-up on light stretching (no longer than 15 seconds per stretch).

When stretching, do not bounce or force your body into a stretch; doing so may strain your muscles. In fact, stretching too forcefully or too quickly can activate a "stretch reflex," which increases muscle tension and resists the stretch. If stretching causes discomfort, you may be able to minimize it (but not eliminate it entirely) by using a roller or ball or by implementing certain breathing and relaxation techniques. If flexibility is a weak area for you, remember to get the blood flowing by engaging in light aerobic activity before stretching.

Remember also that a muscle you think is tight may not be the problem. For example, joint restrictions in your pelvis can cause increased tension throughout your hips and legs. In another example, the calf muscles cross the knee joint, which means that restriction in this area may make it difficult to straighten your knee. And while your hamstrings may in fact be tight, the tightness of interconnecting muscle groups may be the bigger problem.

SUMMARY

Attending one's first hip-hop class can be a bit overwhelming. Participants may feel nervous and may wonder what to wear, what to bring, where to stand, or what to do. Having read this chapter, you can now feel more relaxed and prepared for the experience. You are now aware of appropriate clothing and footwear, and you know what to carry in your bag. You also understand the importance of preparing both mentally and physically, and you know that adequate preparation can help you make the most of your experience in dance class. Even so, before you jump into class, read chapter 3 to find out about key considerations for safety and health.

To find supplementary materials for this chapter, such as learning activities, e-journal assignments, and web links, visit the web resource online.

Chapter 3

Safety and Health

Hip-hop dance is generally a fun and safe activity. However, as with any physical endeavor, injuries sometimes occur. Fortunately, you can prevent many of them by taking appropriate safety precautions and developing your understanding of basic principles of movement, nutrition, and anatomy.

For that purpose, this chapter examines studio safety, including ways to create the best environment to minimize joint and muscle stress and keep the studio free of injury-causing obstacles. It also addresses basic anatomy, proper alignment, and how the human body is designed to move. In addition, because injuries cannot always be avoided, the chapter covers common injuries and simple first aid techniques to speed recovery. Finally, so that you know how to prepare and fuel your body for the strenuous movement required in hip-hop dance, this chapter discusses proper fitness and conditioning, nutrition, hydration, and rest. When you care for your body, you enhance your productivity.

STUDIO SAFETY

Many dance studios are multipurpose facilities that cater to a variety of dance or exercise classes. Some dance classes are also taught in shared facilities, such as a gymnasium. No matter the type of space you are in, safety is an essential consideration. Your teacher is responsible for the safety of the dance space and can provide you with instructions related to federal, state, and local codes that address various emergency and safety situations. The overall goal should always be to take appropriate safety and health measures; in fact, you should be just as committed to maintaining your health and safety as you are to developing your technique and performance.

Dance studios are busy places where large groups of people come and go between classes. Therefore, for your personal safety, and to protect your belongings, you should always be aware of your surroundings, including the facility's entrances and exits. Know the evacuation routes from all parts of the facility, including the studio, the locker room, and the building as a whole. In addition, learn where to go in case of emergencies such as earthquakes and tornado warnings.

Floors

In most dance studios, you will find that the flooring is covered with a PVC (polyvinyl chloride) surface. This vinyl covering is referred to as "marley," after the British company that originally produced it. Marley has become a popular surface for multiple genres of dance, including modern and ballet, but it poses a grave safety concern for hip-hop dancers, who typically perform in rubber-soled sneakers. Dancing in sneakers can stress the knees, and engaging in hip-hop dance on vinyl flooring can cause shin splints, which are known in medical circles as medial tibial stress syndrome.

In contrast, a **sprung floor** absorbs shocks, thus giving it a softer feel (see figure 3.1). This type of flooring is characterized by a suspended wood floor elevated above an original structural floor. If your studio does *not* have wooden flooring, then I suggest wearing a pair of socks over your sneakers to give yourself a smoother surface on which to move.

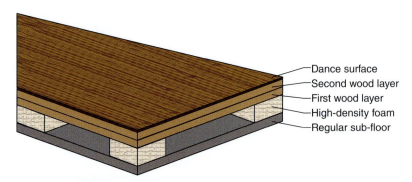

Dance surface
Second wood layer
First wood layer
High-density foam
Regular sub-floor

Figure 3.1 Sprung floor.

In addition, whatever the flooring, wear flat-soled sneakers. In other words, avoid sneakers that feature spiky or rubbery bits under the sole, which can increase your risk of injury as they may restrict smooth transitions of movement creating a pulling or forcible movement around the ankle or knee joints.

If your studio hosts multiple classes on the same floor, bring a separate pair of sneakers for use only in the studio in order to help keep the surface clean for students in other classes who might dance barefoot. Every dancer is responsible for ensuring the safety of the dance space. If you track in dirt, wipe it up. If you spill water, dry it up. Be courteous and help care for your dance space and its surroundings.

> **SAFETY TIP**
>
> Always warm up, and exercise caution when dancing. Performing hip-hop dance with cold or tight muscles is *not* advised. Tight muscles in the foot and ankle are less able to absorb the shock of high-impact activity. They will loosen up, however, if you begin with some light-intensity dancing.

PERSONAL SAFETY

When you take a dance class, you participate in vigorous physical activity with as many as 30 other students whose bodies are moving—sometimes very quickly—in, through, and around the space. Therefore, you must take measures to ensure your own personal safety and help ensure the safety of others in the studio.

As discussed in chapter 2, personal safety begins with your attire and grooming. For instance, before class, remove any jewelry, which can come off when you are dancing and possibly injure you or others. In addition, if you have long hair, secure it so that it does not obstruct your view or distract you or other students as you move.

Personal Space

Your **spatial awareness** plays an important role in safety and enjoyment, both for yourself and for your classmates. It includes your awareness of your own body and of the physical space of the studio. Whether you are remaining in one spot or moving across the floor, manage your **personal space**

The Al B.

ACTIVITY

DETERMINING YOUR PERSONAL SPACE

Stand in a place with no barriers to movement. Extend your arms overhead, then out to the sides of your body. Extend each leg forward, then to the side, and then to the back. Finally, turn yourself around. In this way, you outline a somewhat spherical space that indicates the shape and amount of space you will need in order to execute movements. Think about moving within this sphere when you move in side-to-side and forward-and-backward patterns in the middle of the studio and when moving in groups of two or three in a line, whether across the floor or on a diagonal path.

SAFETY TIP

When dancing with others, make a habit of checking your personal space before and during an exercise or combination. In the center, use your peripheral vision to see objects or people on either side outside of your direct line of vision.

intentionally so that you have room to perform leg, arm, and body extensions without infringing on a neighbor's space.

Personal Health Information

Personal health information is just that: personal. You are not necessarily obligated to tell everyone in class if have had an injury or surgery or if you have a chronic health condition that might affect your physical performance or the health of your peers. You should, however, tell your teacher. Your teacher should be aware of any chronic condition or disease (such as asthma, diabetes, or epilepsy) in order to be prepared for any possible emergency. To protect privacy and enable an appropriate response, teachers usually encourage students to see them for such conversations either just before or just after the first class meeting.

BASIC ANATOMY

Before you can understand movement in dance, you must understand the structure and function of the human body. The bones, muscles, tendons, and ligaments form the foundation for movement. Understanding their structure and function will help you protect your health and safety and minimize your risk of injury.

Skeletal System

Like an automobile, your body is supported by a frame, which in this case is your skeleton (see figure 3.2). The human skeleton includes 206 bones, which assist in voluntary movement and protect vital organs (Clippinger, 2016). It is divided into the **axial skeleton** (central upright axis), which includes the skull, vertebral column, sternum, and ribs, and the **appendicular skeleton**, which includes the limbs.

Bones are often linked to form joints, of which there are three types—fibrous, cartilaginous, and synovial—based on the connective tissue holding them together (Clippinger, 2016). **Fibrous joints** are held together tightly and thus allow little or

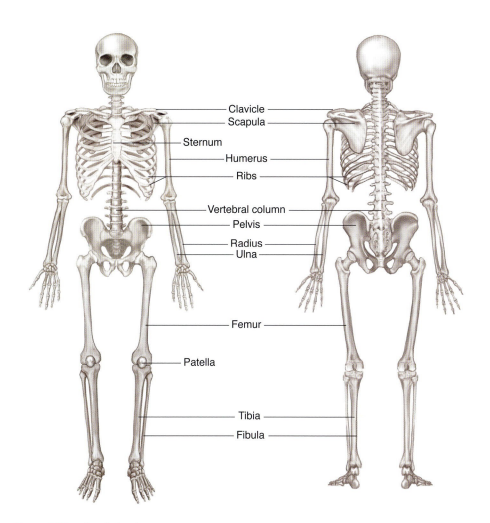

Figure 3.2 The skeletal system.

no true movement; examples include the sutures in the skull. In contrast, as the name suggests, **cartilaginous joints** are joined by cartilage, which is designed to provide shock absorption, as is the case with the vertebrae. Finally, **synovial joints**, such as the knee, allow for the most freedom of movement and make up the most common type of joint in the human body.

The skeletal system accomplishes three major functions:

1. Supporting the body
2. Protecting delicate internal organs
3. Providing attachment sites for muscles and organs

Bones are made up of different types of tissue:

DID YOU KNOW?

I refer to the axial skeleton as the rhythm section of the body. It includes many parts that can indicate rhythms as you hear them in the music. Once you become more advanced at hip-hop dance, you can isolate certain parts of the axial skeleton to express certain rhythms. This is not so much the axial skeleton as it relates to the muscles and organs in the torso as it is the diaphragm, lungs, articulation of the spine, abdominals, pectoral muscles, trapezius, or sternocleidomastoid (paired muscles in the neck).

- **Compact tissue** is a substance that is dense and hard.
- **Cancellous tissue** is the sponge-like interior tissue.
- **Subchondral tissue** is the smooth tissue at the ends of bones (and is covered by another type of tissue, called *cartilage*).

Muscular System

Movement cannot take place without muscles. Skeletal muscles, which account for as much as 40 percent of body weight, are attached to bones (Clippinger, 2016). In functional terms, the muscular system is a network of tissues that produce tension on the bones in order to cause joint movement (see figure 3.3). More specifically, the body is

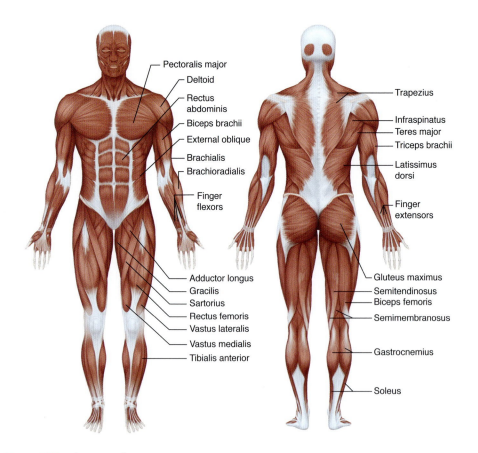

Figure 3.3 The muscular system.

propelled through space by the muscular actions of contraction and relaxation. The human body includes 434 muscles, of which 75 pairs are responsible for body movements. The names of these muscles are rooted in Latin and Greek.

Muscles can contract in various ways. **Dynamic (isotonic) muscle contraction** occurs when the length of the involved muscle changes (Baechle & Earle, 2003). It can take either of two forms (see figure 3.4): **Concentric muscle contraction** involves shortening of the muscle and visible joint movement, whereas **eccentric muscle contraction** involves tension that lengthens the muscle.

To produce a given movement, the involved muscles work together as each plays a certain role. When contracted, a mover or *agonist* muscle produces the desired joint movement. Meanwhile, an *antagonist* muscle produces an opposite action; specifically, it usually relaxes while the mover contracts. The antagonist supports the body part against forces related to muscle contraction. Thus muscles must work together to produce movements that are both precise and smooth.

Thus muscles form the body's contractile tissue system. Within that general description, they can be classified as either skeletal, cardiac, or smooth. In any case, their function is to produce force; thus, in addition to moving the body in visible ways, they maintain posture and circulate blood throughout the body. When you want to move your joints, your muscles spring into action. At any point, muscles can take on different roles, depending on what motion is required.

Muscles are made up of many smaller parts. Specifically, like the rest of your body, your muscles are made up of individual cells. These cells, or muscle fibers, come together to form fascicles—that is, groups or bundles of muscle fibers—which make up a given muscle.

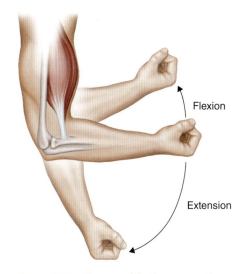

Flexion

Extension

Figure 3.4 Flexion of the biceps involves concentric muscle contraction, whereas extension of the biceps involves eccentric muscle contraction.

BASIC KINESIOLOGY

Although the acute trauma involved in dramatic injuries may stand out in our minds, the majority of dance injuries result from overload, or recurrent trauma, and from biomechanical factors (Clippinger, 2016). Therefore, if you understand basic kinesiology, or human movement, then you can minimize your risk of dance injuries and help yourself heal when an injury does occur. To that end, this section explains terms related to movement. This understanding also makes you a more informed dancer. Dancers (and other athletes) need to understand these terms in order to communicate effectively about injuries or concerns with physicians, physical therapists, athletic trainers, and massage therapists.

Anatomical Position

In addition to common words such as *bone*, *skeleton*, and *muscle*—which are part of your everyday vocabulary—certain anatomical terms can help you understand the workings of the artistic instrument that is your body. To begin with, the front of the body is referred to as **anterior**, the back of the body as **posterior**, the parts closest to the midline of the body as **medial**, and the parts farthest from the midline as **lateral**. These terms provide a way for scientists to map the body by creating a sort of compass for navigating it. Thus they help health professionals be specific when talking about the body: Is the pain in your knee medial (on the inside part) or posterior (in the back of the knee)? They also help create landmarks on the body. For instance, even when your leg is turned out so that the front of your knee faces to the side, the front part is still the anterior portion.

Figure 3.5 Anatomical position.

Similarly, in order to understand movement, you must first understand basic anatomical terminology. The universal starting position is referred to as the **anatomical position** (figure 3.5). It is an erect standing position with the feet forward, the arms down by the sides, and the palms forward with the thumbs pointing outward and the fingers extended. In contrast, the **prone position** is characterized by lying facedown on the front of the body, and the **supine position** is characterized by lying faceup on the back.

Connective Tissue

People often think of muscles as being attached directly to bones, but in fact these attachments are part of a complex system of connective tissue. Specifically, muscles are attached to bones by **tendons**, and bones are attached to other bones by **ligaments**. Both of these kinds of connective tissue—as well as others—play key roles in gaining flexibility, developing strength, maintaining stability, and executing clear and safe dance movements.

Joint Movements

Synovial joints permit the following basic joint movements:

- **Flexion**—decreasing joint angle, as in bending the elbow (figure 3.6*a*)
- **Extension**—increasing joint angle, as in straightening the elbow (figure 3.6*a*)
- **Hyperextension**—extending past natural position, as in bending backward
- **Abduction**—moving away from the midline (figure 3.6*b*)
- **Adduction**—moving toward the midline (figure 3.6*b*)
- **Rotation**—turning the anterior surface outward (external rotation) or turning the anterior surface inward (internal rotation; figure 3.6*c*)
- **Circumduction**—movement that creates a complete circle and combines flexion, abduction, extension, and adduction (figure 3.6*c*).

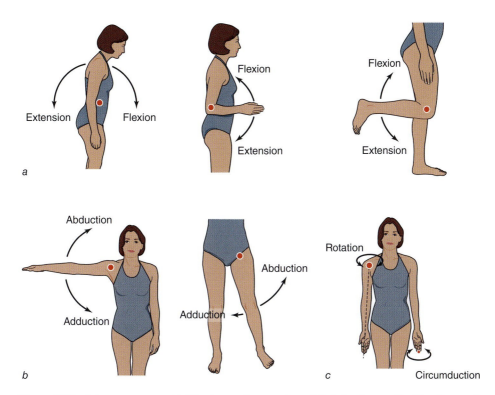

Figure 3.6 Joint movements: *(a)* flexion and extension; *(b)* abduction and adduction; and *(c)* rotation and circumduction.

Joint stability is the ability of a joint to withstand mechanical shocks or movements without injury. It is provided by the following factors: the shape of the component, the ligaments that guide the joint through its range of motion, the vacuum created in the joint, and the extensibility of the involved muscles and tendons.

Much of what is known about preventing dance injuries has been learned through the expertise of dance scientists, physical therapists, physicians, orthopedic surgeons, and sport trainers. Therefore, you will benefit from listening to their advice about preventing, diagnosing, and treating dance injuries. In contrast, although your teacher and fellow dancers may have personal experience with injury, they are not medical professionals. Therefore, for any concerns about your health or healing, you should always consult a health professional who is familiar with the unique needs of dancers.

PREVENTING COMMON DANCE INJURIES

Every physical activity comes with a risk of injury. Both acute and chronic injuries can occur for many reasons, including lack of body awareness, poor dance technique, overuse of certain muscles, attempts to use advanced technique before being ready, lack of appropriate warm-up, and studio or floor hazards. If this list seems overwhelming, remember that the first step in preventing injury is simply to take care of your own body through good posture, correct use of muscles, and body awareness. To help with these key points, strictly follow your instructor's advice for properly executing each movement. Common injuries in hip-hop dance include ankle sprains, knee problems, neck strains, and shin splints. Acute injuries often result from landing incorrectly and rolling the ankle after a jump or leap.

Ankle Sprains

Ankle sprains are perhaps the most common types of ankle injury for dancers. **Sprains** occur when the ligaments in or around a joint are stretched or moved beyond their maximum range of motion. The force causes some of the ligament's fibers to stretch, or even tear, thus rendering the joint unstable. Like shin splints, sprains usually cause significant pain.

Sprains are sometimes graded into three degrees of severity:

1. Microscopic tears and stretching but no visible tearing
2. Some torn fibers but ligament still intact
3. Ligament tear in which the structure is completely ruptured, resulting in significant disability in the affected joint

Injury Prevention Tips

- Always warm up before class.
- Try to ensure that your knees and toes always point in the same direction. If they are properly aligned, you maintain strength and proper structure and are less likely to suffer ankle injuries.

Neck Strains

A **strain** can result from moving your body past its natural range of motion, overusing a movement, or overstretching a muscle or tendon. For instance, dance moves that call for excessive head movement can easily strain a dancer's neck muscles, especially if the dancer does not properly warm up or use the full spine when arching. The Nae Nae, for instance, uses neck muscles that must be warmed up before repeating the motion too many times.

Injury Prevention Tips

- Keep your neck muscles strong by doing short sets of strengthening and stretching exercise throughout the class and during the day. For instance, tucking your chin to your chest helps warm up the muscles that pull your head into alignment over your shoulders.
- Stay hydrated. Drinking lots of water during class hydrates the intervertebral discs—the spongy structures that lie between the vertebrae in your neck. These discs are made up mostly of water, and staying well hydrated helps keep them pliable and strong.
- Identify and remedy poor posture, which can cause neck pain by straining the muscles and ligaments that support the neck, thus resulting in injury over time.

Shin Splints

Shin splints involve microtears in muscle or bone (see figure 3.7). Although anyone can experience them, they may be more likely to occur in a dancers who have tight calves and short Achilles tendons. Shin splints indicate stress in the muscles and other tissues next to the tibia, and they are usually extremely painful. They can be caused by overuse, improper technique, or a sudden increase (or stop) in activity.

Injury Prevention Tips

- Avoid sudden increase or decrease in movement.
- Include pointing, flexing, and rotating the feet during your warm-up and cool-down.
- Stretch the calves regularly, especially after repeated hopping or jumping.
- Massage the legs with down strokes.
- Take a hot bath. You can also sit in a hot tub for three minutes and then in an ice bath for another three minutes.

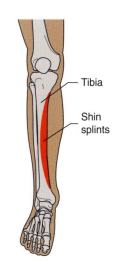

Figure 3.7 Shin splints.

TREATING COMMON DANCE INJURIES

Treatment for all injuries begins with the **PRICED** approach: protection, rest, ice, compression, elevation, and diagnosis.

- Protection. Don't try to tough it out! Doing so will likely cause further damage to your tissues.
- Rest. Stop dancing so the injury can heal. While you are resting, observe what you feel. Is it a dull ache? A stabbing or throbbing pain? What is the precise location of your injury? Did it happen on the first repetition or on the tenth?
- Ice. Applying ice to an injury cannot hurt you, and it should always be your first line of defense. Ice reduces swelling and thus can begin to alleviate pain. Ice the injury for 10 to 12 minutes, then remove the ice for 12 minutes before reapplying for another 10 to 12 minutes. Ice and rest three times. To prevent skin burns, put a towel or two or three layers of fabric between your skin and the ice.
- Compression. For certain injuries, you can help reduce swelling by constricting the injured area by wrapping it with an elastic bandage. If you do not have one, use a t-shirt, bandana, scarf, or anything that can be tied around

TECHNIQUE TIP

If you suffer an injury that prevents you from dancing, continue to attend class as an observer. Take written notes and turn them in to the instructor at the end of class to show that you are still developing your eye for observing movement.

the area. Do not wrap it as tightly as possible; just make the wrapping snug. If you feel a throbbing sensation, unwrap the bandage and rewrap it more loosely. Complete the compression step only if you have an acute injury with swelling. This treatment is not needed for dance injuries that develop slowly with no apparent swelling.

- Elevation. Raise the injured area above the heart to help reduce swelling. Again, this step is necessary only for an acute injury with swelling.

- Diagnosis. Within 24 to 48 hours, see a medical professional—that is, a doctor, physical therapist, or athletic trainer.

Once you receive a clear diagnosis, the next phase of your treatment can begin. This phase will involve working with your physician to develop a recovery plan. You may also work with a physical therapist who understands dance mechanics and can evaluate your recovery path and your progress. Keep your dance teacher informed of the recovery plan so that he or she can help you slowly return to dance activities as they become appropriate for you.

WARMING UP

Warming up properly can help you prevent injuries in hip-hop class. In addition to providing physical benefits, a good warm-up gives you a chance to clear your mind so that you can focus in class. When your mind is focused on the task at hand, you are less prone to accidents. A warm-up is especially important if the outside temperature is cold, because cold muscles are more prone to injury; however, a good

Freestyling.

warm-up prepares your body to perform safely in class. After you have warmed up, you may also want to lightly stretch your muscles in order to improve flexibility. This is also a time to incorporate any additional warm-up that is called for if you have had an injury and the affected body part needs extra attention.

Your teacher can help you create a personal warm-up, or you can create one yourself based on what you have learned in class. In general, you should begin your warm-up with simple mobilization movements, such as progress from head to toe. Then move on to gradually increasing your body's cardiorespiratory activity, e.g., lifting the leg up and placing it back down to running in place. If you have a preexisting injury or alignment issue, inform your teacher and consult a doctor or physical therapist before attempting any stretches. Discontinue any exercise that causes pain or severe discomfort and consult a medical expert.

UNDERSTANDING FITNESS

Hip-hop dance is both an art form and a physical activity, and it requires both physical and mental fitness. In class, your movements raise your body temperature and you experience a physical workout. While your body works out, your mind prepares you for your next movements, solves problems, and retains a movement memory for you to review and analyze in order to prepare for the next class. Understanding the relationship between hip-hop dance and fitness can help you enhance your health for better dance performance and enhance your dance performance for better health.

Principles of Fitness

Principles used in fitness and sport also apply to dance. In particular, the **FITT principle**—which addresses frequency, intensity, time, and type of activity—and the overload principle can help you create an appropriate exercise program that progresses safely. Here are brief descriptions of these factors:

- *Frequency.* Most academic hip-hop classes meet multiple times per week, typically with one day between meetings. This break gives your body time to rest and recuperate before undertaking the same type of strenuous activity again.
- *Intensity.* This term refers to how hard you exercise during a period of physical activity. As your hip-hop course progresses, the intensity rises with the increase in the number and complexity of movements.
- *Time.* The duration of each class period may not vary, but you can still vary the length of time for which you are active during class and during your practices outside of class.
- *Type.* Hip-hop class includes cardiorespiratory activity, as well as muscle-building exercises and flexibility work.
- *Overload.* This principle refers to working a targeted muscle group beyond what it has previously done in order to develop strength. The body responds to more difficult demands by adapting itself; depending on the type of overload, it increases strength, endurance, or both.

The type of overload is affected by the frequency, intensity, time, and type of exercise in which you engage. Creating healthy adaptations in the body is a slow, continuous process that requires effort. The body must be given time to create gradual increases in strength and endurance.

Strength and Conditioning Considerations

As a hip-hop dancer, you need a strong core of muscles to augment the work you do in class. Some dancers supplement their work in class by performing push-ups, sit-ups, and other exercises (such as Pilates and yoga) for strength and flexibility outside of class. When doing such exercises, focus on strengthening the core while keeping the body properly aligned. You can also use weight training to increase your muscular strength and help you rehabilitate from injury. These and other types of activities can help you improve your general health, enhance your dance performance, and avoid or recover from injury.

NUTRITION, HYDRATION, AND REST

Proper nutrition and hydration can improve your physical performance and your short-term and long-term health. In order to understand how these factors can improve your dance performance, you must first understand how they relate to the basics of exercise physiology. Effective dance training and recovery also depend on proper rest.

Nutrition

Like an automobile, your body requires fuel in order to move; in other words, human movement begins with the chemical bonds of food. These chemical bonds, called **macronutrients**, consist of carbohydrate, protein, and fat. Although protein is important for tissue repair and regulatory purposes, carbohydrate and fat are the primary suppliers of energy.

Carbohydrate is digested in the small intestine, absorbed, and then transported to the liver and muscles, where it is stored as glycogen. The liver releases glycogen into the bloodstream in the form of glucose in order to maintain normal blood-glucose levels. Glucose is used by the brain and the skeletal muscles and can serve as an immediate energy source. Because carbohydrate is the primary fuel used during physical activity, you must consume it on a daily basis. Trained athletes and dancers should consume 5 to 10 grams of carbohydrate per kilogram of body weight (Dunford, 2006).

Proteins are complex organic compounds. Their basic structure consists of a chain of amino acids, and they are important for tissue repair and regulatory purposes. Protein-containing foods can be categorized as providing either complete or incomplete proteins. Complete proteins contain all nine essential amino acids; examples include those found in animal products (such as fish, eggs, and milk) and some non-animal products (such as quinoa). In contrast, incomplete proteins—such as those found in most beans, nuts, and grains—lack one or more of the essential amino acids but can be consumed in combination to form a complete protein. Thus vegans and vegetarians can consume a combination of beans, nuts, and grains to achieve their daily protein requirements.

According to the Institute of Medicine's Dietary Reference Intake, the protein requirement for dancers is the same as that for adults in general, which is 0.8 gram per kilogram of body weight per day (Dunford, 2006). Although endurance and resistance-trained athletes may need more, dancers are usually not included in those categories.

Many dancers fear the word *fat*. However, fat is essential: It serves as a major energy source, helps maintain body temperature, protects body organs, contributes to the satiety value of foods, and aids in the delivery and absorption of fat-soluble vitamins. Dietary fat is digested into fatty acids, absorbed in the small intestine, and stored in the form of triglycerides in adipose (fatty) tissue. Fatty acids can be used immediately for energy.

Hydration

When you are dehydrated, you may feel fatigued, find it hard to concentrate, and even be at risk of injury. For peak performance, you must be properly hydrated before, during, and after a dance class or performance. To optimize your fluid intake, drink extra water during the 10 to 15 minutes before class begins, and consume water regularly during class. Avoid drinking alcohol within 72 hours before or after training.

> ### DID YOU KNOW?
>
> Coffee, soda, alcohol, and sugary beverages may be tempting, but they offer little, if any, nutritional value and can contribute to dehydration. Replacing one or more of these drinks with water during the day will help you stay properly hydrated and reduce your consumption of empty calories.

Rest

To prepare for dance class, you should be well rested. Along with proper nutrition and hydration, adequate rest supports body recovery and revitalization. When muscles are overloaded, they need rest in order to rebuild themselves. Your mind also needs rest for optimal functioning. When you don't get enough rest, you become less alert and more prone to accidents. If you have trouble sleeping or feel too anxious to rest, learn some relaxation techniques and pace yourself during the day so that your body and mind have time to rest.

SUMMARY

Hip-hop dance is an exhilarating and fun activity. This chapter has introduced you to basic anatomy and kinesiology; injury prevention and care; and the importance of nutrition, hydration, and rest. Understanding the basic terms introduced here can help you communicate effectively with your physician, physical therapist, athletic trainer, or massage therapist. It also helps you understand your body and how to enhance its health and safety.

Hip-hop dance is generally safe, but performing any physical activity carries a possibility of injury. If you become injured, knowing the nature of typical injuries can help you assess your injury and determine whether to seek medical advice. Most discomfort can be alleviated using the PRICED method. Your body is your vehicle for movement and expression. When you understand how to properly fuel, hydrate, and move it, you can keep it toned, fit, and less prone to injury.

To find supplementary materials for this chapter, such as learning activities, e-journal assignments, and web links, visit the web resource online.

Chapter 4

Basics of Hip-Hop Technique

Learning hip-hop dance is a whole-brain activity that engages the emotional body, spiritual body, physical body, mental body, sensual body, and **fluid body** (which enables and expresses steady and continuous movement). You have to use your whole body to respond to the music: your ears listen, your eyes see the shapes, and your body expresses the movement. In this way, your body and the music become one. As dancers, we make music visible; by watching you move, your audience can experience the music on a deeper level. When you physicalize what you hear, you turn your body into a visual representation of the sound.

You can develop your creativity in dance by increasing your body's strength and flexibility and by understanding how to use polyrhythm and polycentrism in fluid isolations of the neck, shoulders, torso, wrists, hips, butt, and feet. Of course, these skills won't be perfected during your first week in class; they will, however, improve over time as you develop your kinesthetic awareness and muscle memory. You will do so by repeating exercises and steps to various songs and rhythm patterns. Through this process, you will develop your basic understanding of

musicality—how you listen to music—and your ability to interpret the sensuality, expressiveness, and sheer joy of music along with the rhythm, melody, harmony, multilayered qualities, and the groove.

This ability to interpret sound will become clear in **call-and-response** interactions. Call-and-response is a form of communication rooted in African cultural tradition that involves both verbal and nonverbal actions and reactions. Hip-hop music is made in the call-and-response tradition, with the rapper (the caller) leading the audience to respond. For example, the rapper might say, "When I say *hip*, you say *hop* . . . Hip!" And the audience will respond with "hop!"

At dance practices, the music is the caller, and the dancer responds *with* the beat instead of after it. One of the ways in which dancers use call-and-response in class is through the verbal cues *Ago* (ah-go) and *Ame* (ah-may). *Ago* is a call for attention, and *Ame* is its response. Thus the teacher says "Ago," meaning "listen or attend," to which the students reply "Ame," meaning "I am [we are] listening."

There is no single, officially correct concept or approach for teaching hip-hop. Because it is a social form of dance, the dances are open to interpretation, which allows dancers to celebrate their individual voices. Thus your background or your first exposure to a dance may determine the names you associate with it, how you perform it, and even the songs you play with it. At the same time, though each dance is individualized, the structures and characteristics of hip-hop are rooted in African concepts and traditions. In *African American Dance: An Illustrated History* (2007), Barbara Glass refers to these characteristics as the African Movement Vocabulary, which stands in contrast to the fixed steps and lifted torsos of European dance forms.

More specifically, African and African-diasporic dances tend to focus on angular bending of the arms, legs, torso, shoulders, hips, and butt; they often include scuffing, stamping, hopping, and asymmetrical yet fluid movement. Their orientation to the earth—with knees bent and torso leaning forward from the waist—creates a sense of groundedness and of giving energy to and receiving energy from the earth. Glass (2007) also identifies the following important elements in these dances: improvisation, circle and line formations, community, polyrhythm, percussion, pantomime, holding something in hand (such as a hat or towel), and competition. Although no single book can explain everything there is to know about any form of dance, these characteristics are explored in this text as a way to help you discover and nurture yourself and your story.

BEATS APPROACH

The following discussion presents my approach and methodology for teaching hip-hop dance, which I refer to as BEATS. This acronymic name reflects the marriage between music, the body, and movement principles. The approach draws on neurological philosophies of awareness that engage feelings (visceral reactions), emotions (feelings made visible), and responsiveness, as well as musical concepts and African American cultural characteristics.

B for Body

We begin by using the body to represent musical notation. To do so, you must first find the groove. Whether you are bouncing, rocking, or doing a two-step, there is a smoothness or groove in the movement (the term grooving refers to moving smoothly or deftly). The groove is found in the articulation of the neck, shoulders, spine, elbows, wrists, hips, knees, and ankles. In these areas, you can express the notes, time, dynamics, rhythms, tonality, phrasing, and space that you hear in the music.

When looking at the physical body as a musical instrument, the axial skeleton (see chapter 3) can be seen as the rhythm section—for example, bass, drums, piano, and guitar. More specifically, intrinsic rhythmic play can be expressed through the use of the spine, the arrangement of the muscles, and the fluidity of the breath. In contrast, the appendicular skeleton, which includes the limbs, gives a more general impression of rhythmic fluidity. Reasons for engaging in grounded or heavy movement come from the musical scale. When the music uses low tones like a heavy bass or kick drum, this is an opportunity to be low or grounded with your movement. Higher notes on the scale, or perhaps wind instruments like a flute that give a light or airy quality, is an opportunity to explore tall, floating or jumping movements. The objective is to convey the mood of the notes through physical expression. The directness, dynamics, and sustainability of your movement are examined in the notes: accents, polyrhythm, and so on (you are allowed to shift where these are expressed in your body).

E for Emotion

Music can affect us positively or negatively and can awaken the conscious self in each of us. In applying the word *emotion* to our purpose here, we can think of the *e* as indicating energy, the *mo* as indicating ephemerality (that is, the quality of lasting only a short time), and *tion* as indicating action. Altogether, then, we can view *emotion* as referring to the energy behind our short-lived actions, which is expressed in our interpretations of musical character through our dancing. Music can stimulate a myriad of emotions, from those of a free adventurous spirit to those of a chilling or gripping sensation. The power of emotion in music resonates through our inner selves and may help us understand not only what we dance but also why.

A for Attitude and Aesthetic

Attitude gives emotion a physicality, a face, a behavior, and a poise. You create a style and character to express your individuality, self-confidence, and current mood as manifested by the music. An aesthetic is a set of ideals concerned with nurturing a pleasing appearance, as well as appreciation of the beauty created through the marriage of music and the body.

T for Tone and Time

Tone consists of the overall quality of a musical note or vocal sound; for instance, it includes the brightness, deepness, or intensity of the musical body. **Time** is the

Whole note

Half note

Quarter note

Eighth note

Sixteenth note

Figure 4.1 Musical note value symbols.

rhythmic pattern and tempo in music. It can represent the past, the present, or the future and can be expressed either through sudden or sustained movements or through stillness. In practical application, time is expressed in the duration of each note (see figure 4.1):

- A whole note is sustained to fill an entire measure of music, which in hip-hop usually contains four beats.
- A half note takes up two beats.
- A quarter note takes up one beat.
- An eighth note takes up half of a quarter note (you can count eighth notes by saying "one, and, two, and . . .").
- A sixteenth note takes up half of an eighth note (count "one, e, and, a, two, e, and, a . . .").

S for Space or Sound

Space—mental and physical, internal and external, available or occupied—is the playground for exploration. It is either direct or indirect, meaning you can have an intentional or unintentional pattern, as perceived through our sensory faculties. The BEATS approach reimagines how we use space in the room, on the stage, and between the notes. Your body is the bridge between yourself and the contents of the space you are in, and it is accessible through your imagination and through dance. For example, if the space includes a chair or table, don't just dance around it or near it—use it! Bring the object into your dance to develop a narrative in real time. Even if the space is empty, you can use pantomime to suggest that something is there.

All music is made up of sounds and silences. Sounds are vibrations that connect us to the essence of life. Whether deriving from the spoken word, from a music speaker, or from the live playing of an instrument, sounds create pressure waves that compress air molecules as they travel outward, thus creating frequencies of sound. These frequencies can resonate with our bodies. You may have seen dramatizations of the fact that the vibrations created by a singer can cause a glass to shatter by eliciting strong vibrations in it. In the same way, music causes reactions in our bodies—for example, the sensation of goose bumps. Music can also include silences, which can evoke ideas and convey impressions; similarly, as dancers, we can create dynamics and expectations by being still, e.g., when Michael Jackson would stand still on stage, which is a type of silence. We can also create sound through body percussion and the use of rhythmic movements inside the silence of the music.

The BEATS approach to dancing engages the whole brain—both the analytical and the creative dimensions—for the purpose of outlining ways in which dancers can use music to tell their stories for either personal enjoyment or performance. This process involves three basic elements: feelings, emotions, and responsiveness.

Feelings are visceral reactions to the music, emotions are feelings made visible, and responsiveness involves the awareness that enables you to put your feelings and emotions into dance actions in real time.

ALIGNMENT AND STANCE

Good alignment involves correctly positioning your body parts in relation to each other. For most hip-hop dances, you will begin in fundamental position, or fundamental stance (see figure 4.2). Essentially, you will stand up straight with your feet hip-width apart (or a bit farther) and your knees slightly bent. Make sure your knees are aligned over your toes, with your knees and toes pointing forward; your knees should not be twisted in either direction. Your shoulders are stacked directly on top of your hips as you begin. The center line is a straight vertical line that separates the right and left halves of your body.

SAFETY TIP

Be continuously aware of your alignment. If it is compromised, your safety can be compromised as well. In particular, keep your knees aligned with your toes at all times to avoid straining the tendons in your knees. If you have difficulty with maintaining correct alignment, consult a dance scientist or physician for a postural assessment. An expert can help you make adaptations for any anatomical abnormalities.

Figure 4.2   Dancer standing with correct alignment in fundamental position.

ISOLATION GROOVES

Humans are musical beings who can entrain (to fall into synchronization with) to a rhythmic beat (Mannes, 2011). In fact, life itself is a rhythmic journey; the cycle of our emotions, the flow of our blood, and the way we walk and talk are all rhythmical. As explained earlier, dance begins with the groove, the smoothness that one displays in expressing the rhythm: "The feel of the groove is a central element of the body's motor-intentional engagement with rhythmic elements of music" (Roholt, 2014, p. 105). Find your groove to define your move.

The groove is the nuance between the sounds and silence created by the musicians; it is a pulse that is both physical and acoustic. Physically, the groove is found in the range of motion using the neck, shoulders, chest, spine, hips, elbows, wrists, fingers, knees, and ankles. Acoustically, the groove exists between the notes, articulation, technique, feel, dynamics, rhythm, tone, phrasing, and space of the music. Other elements include harmony, loudness, and tempo. The degree to which we understand these elements depends on cognitive transmission; the brain processes them not as separate components but as a whole. Some areas of the brain that are involved in this process are identified in figure 4.3.

These cognitive elements become both emotional and spiritual as they are translated into your dancing. For example, the James Brown song "Get Up, Get Into It, Get Involved" partakes of the call-and-response tradition. Brown is calling for us to get on our feet. Once we are up, we get into it (the groove) and by getting into it we find ourselves involved in the whole-body experience. The groove in the dance is the steadiness of our movement, the smooth flow with the tempo of the music.

In isolation grooves, the articulation of the spine and the placement of the muscles allows for a fluidity that does not exist anywhere else in the body. Remember that the axial skeleton is the body's rhythm section. While focusing on a particular part of the body, try to allow the rest of the body to enjoy some movement. For example, add a side-to-side two-step while practicing isolations in the upper body. During each of the following isolation exercises, pay attention to the total movement—not only when the body aligns with the beat but also when the smoothness exists in between the beat.

ACTIVITY

FINDING THE PULSE

Keeping a steady pulse is important to maintaining the groove and to finding synergy with the tempo of the music. To develop your ability to maintain the pulse, practice by tapping your foot or clapping your hands to songs with various tempos. You can also practice syncopation by tapping or clapping on the second and fourth beats of the music.

TECHNIQUE TIP

Always allow your body to groove. Don't stand stiffly while moving only a selected body part. Allowing your body to groove helps you develop your polyrhythmic and polycentric capabilities.

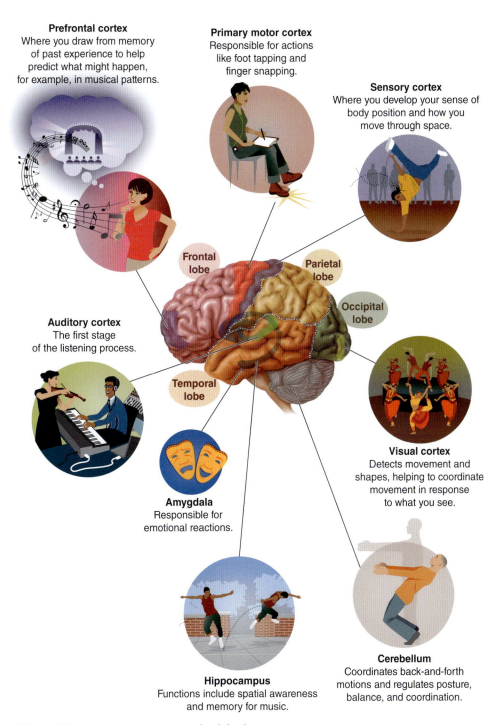

Prefrontal cortex
Where you draw from memory of past experience to help predict what might happen, for example, in musical patterns.

Primary motor cortex
Responsible for actions like foot tapping and finger snapping.

Sensory cortex
Where you develop your sense of body position and how you move through space.

Auditory cortex
The first stage of the listening process.

Visual cortex
Detects movement and shapes, helping to coordinate movement in response to what you see.

Amygdala
Responsible for emotional reactions.

Hippocampus
Functions include spatial awareness and memory for music.

Cerebellum
Coordinates back-and-forth motions and regulates posture, balance, and coordination.

Frontal lobe

Parietal lobe

Occipital lobe

Temporal lobe

Figure 4.3 Brain processes at work while dancing.

▶ Neck Isolations

Neck isolations include a variety of options. For instance, Pecking involves keeping the head in a neutral position and pushing the neck forward or pulling it backward in a steady rhythm in tempo with the song. In contrast, the Say What involves moving the neck to the side in a steady rhythm while keeping the head level, as if you were trying to move the ear over to hear something. Among other options, keeping the head leveled while circling the neck in either direction is referred to as the Oh No You Didn't; tilting the head up and back is the What's Up; tilting the head down and forward is called Yahmean, Nahmean, or Namsayin (for "You know what I mean?" or "You know what I'm saying?"); and rotating the head to the left and then to the right at a slight 40-degree angle is the Neck Rock. Collectively, these movements can be referred to as "tapping the beat" with the neck when done to a specific rhythm.

▶ Shoulder Isolations

The shoulders play a key role in fluidly passing movement from the arms to the torso; they also help you achieve polyrhythmicity. Here are four types of shoulder isolations:

1. Stand with your feet shoulder-width apart and your knees slightly bent. Steadily bounce your shoulders in a downward motion so that they fall on each quarter note, then on each eighth note. Accent notes 2 and 4 by bending your knees. Extension: Try alternating by moving one shoulder front and down (initiating with the clavicle) while the other shoulder goes back and down (initiating with the scapula).

2. Extend your arms out to your sides with your wrists slightly lower than your shoulders. In a shrugging motion, pull your shoulders in to your neck, then outward and down to the start position. Eventually, you want to be able to achieve this shoulder movement with your arms at multiple levels while controlling the motion with your trapezius muscles.

3. Roll both shoulders forward and back, then try alternating one forward and one back. For a slightly harder level of coordination, practice bouncing your left shoulder up and down while rolling your right shoulder forward and then back. Repeat on the opposite side.

4. Beginning in a neutral stance, move your shoulders up in four counts in small pulses, back to neutral in four counts, then down for four counts, and back to neutral in another four counts (attempt all four exercises at various tempos). Next, do the same on a horizontal (transverse) plane by moving your shoulders forward and back rather than up and down. Then try the same exercises while alternating the direction of the shoulders in four counts, then in two counts, and finally back and forth in a steady beat pattern.

Say What (horizontal neck slide).

▶ Torso Isolations

The basis for torso isolations is provided by your breathing. Begin by warming up the lungs, diaphragm, and abdominals through breathing exercises. The goal is to connect to the fluidity and control in your spine, breath, and muscles so that they can relate to the music and movement. You may want to try these exercises while lying down, then while sitting up or in a chair, and finally while standing or walking. This progression will help you note differences and dimensionality in your breathing, as well as any difficulty you may experience.

Lungs

Focusing on your lungs and keeping your head level, place one hand on your chest and the other on your diaphragm. Inhale through your nose and feel your chest and rib cage expand as your diaphragm contracts. Then exhale through your mouth and bring everything back to its neutral position. Breathe in time with music—for example, Keni Burke's "Risin' to the Top," which has a tempo of 94 beats per minute. Using basic musical notation, inhale with the timing of a whole note—four counts then exhale, then four counts down; repeat this pattern three times. Repeat the exercise in the time of a half note (two counts) and then in the time of a quarter note (one count). Next, try pulsing your chest to the beat in an upward motion for two counts of eight while breathing normally through your lungs (do not breath with each pulse).

Diaphragm

First, warm up your diaphragm by making three sounds—"he," "ho," and "ha," each with a sharp "h" sound—in short breath intervals (a pause or break in between each sound). "He" is a wide-mouth sound, "ho" is a round-mouth sound, and "ha" is a tall-mouth sound. Repeat three times. Next, focus your *chi* (Chinese for circulating life force) on your diaphragm, keeping your lungs relaxed. Place one hand on your chest and your index and middle finger at the center of the rib cage on the base of your sternum (see figure 4.4). Your objective is to breathe in by expanding your diaphragm so that you feel a push on your fingers. To practice this expansion, use the same note application (whole, half, and so on) as with the preceding exercise for the lungs.

Figure 4.4 Finding your diaphragm.

Abdominals

Stand in fundamental stance—with your knees slightly bent, your hips neutral (aligned underneath your shoulders, with neither hip lifted or dropped), and your chest lifted—and relax your abdominals. The upper abdominal region is located about 1 inch (2.5 cm) below the sternum. Place your fingertips on the muscle and focus your breath on your upper abdominals, then contract the muscle. To locate the muscle, inhale and exhale sharply. Follow the musical notation from the previous exercises, pushing your upper abdominals forward for a count of four, then two, and finally one; repeat, but this time pull your upper abdominals inward rather than pushing them outward. Then try short pulses in both directions.

Next, place your fingers on your mid abdominals, located at the navel area and repeat same steps for upper abdominals

Next, go down to your lower abdominals by placing your fingers about 1 inch (2.5 cm) below your navel. If you have trouble locating this area, cough or laugh and you will find it. Continuing in the fundamental stance, begin to contract the muscle as you pull it inward. It is okay at first for your hips to rock slightly forward and then release, but eventually you want to achieve this contraction without rocking your hips. Perform the same exercise described for the upper abdominals but keep the upper abdominals still.

Once you feel comfortable with these movements, try rolling your abdominals. In fundamental stance, contract your upper abdominals and then your lower abdominals while keeping the overall abdominal region tight. Next, push your upper abdominals out, followed by your lower abdominals, and then repeat. Take your time; this process should give a nice rolling of the belly. Try reversing the movement—that is, beginning with your lower abdominals. Push them outward, followed by your upper abdominals; then pull your lower abdominals inward, followed by your upper abdominals.

▶ Hip Isolations

Because your hips are controlled by a ball-and-socket joint, they can move in many directions. The following hip isolations are similar to isolations used in jazz dance. In contrast to torso isolations, these movements do not focus on the breath.

Hip Pop

Standing in fundamental stance, contract your left hip upward by engaging your left gluteal muscle; this action should cause your heel to lift. Then contract your pelvis forward, also engaging the gluteal muscles. Next, contract your right hip, then relax your hips back to neutral. Now follow the same pattern used for the torso exercises by popping your hip in each direction, first in counts of eight, then four, and then two. Then alternate from side to side or back and forth with one-counts.

Hip Roll

Standing in fundamental stance, contract your right hip up. Next, contract your lower abs inward and then your left hip up before returning to fundamental stance. Along the way, you will shift the weight from one side to the other in your legs and feet. Focus closely on the isolations of your pelvis as you perform rolls that are small, fluid, and continuous. Then try it in the opposite direction.

Single-Hip Roll

Begin by standing with your weight on your right leg, which is bent slightly more than your left leg. Put your weight on the ball of your right foot with your right heel off the ground. With both knees bent, contract your left hip up, then forward, then down, and then back to neutral, thus making a circle. Focus on the pelvic bone and work toward keeping your shoulders level. Try this sequence in both directions and then on the opposite side.

▶ Counterflow Isolations

Counterflow isolations focus on the neck, torso, and hips (and each exercise is done in eight counts). These isolations can be difficult because they require you to perform simultaneous but separate isolations in different body parts. Begin with the following steps one at a time, and slowly add on the rest.

   1. Stand in fundamental stance. Keep your torso still; to make sure it is not moving, you can place your hands on your chest. This exercise is similar to the Say What neck isolation, but this time, instead of pushing to one side, you move your neck back and forth from the left side all the way to the right side in full range of motion.

   2. Keeping your head completely still, try moving your torso from side to side. Keep your head still; to make sure it is not moving, you can place your hands on either

TECHNIQUE TIP

In counterflow isolations, keep your head level and vertical. Don't lead with your chin or the crown of your head. In addition, keep your movement fluid; do not stop in the middle.

side of your head. Keep your shoulders relaxed and down. Using the breathing exercise from the torso isolation of the lungs, pull your rib cage over to the left and then to the right.

3. Move your neck down and forward for one beat. On the next beat, move your torso down and forward to realign it with your neck; bend at the waist so that only your torso moves. Repeat until your back is parallel to the ground, then rise back up in the same fashion—neck first, then torso.

4. Next, repeat the exercises in this section but once you are parallel to the ground keep your torso still and roll your neck around in the Oh No You Didn't motion. Then, keeping your head still, roll your torso in the same way that you roll your neck. You can also reverse the direction of this movement.

▶ Bouncing

Bouncing in hip-hop dance serves two major roles: First, it is fundamental to the hip-hop aesthetic; second, it helps you transition from one movement to the next without losing the fluidity of the groove. There are four main bounces: drop bounce, East Coast stomp, rock step, and skipping-rope bounce.

Drop Bounce

To perform the drop bounce, stand in fundamental stance. The drop bounce consists of a steady descending and ascending motion (bending with your knees) in time with the quarter notes of the music and sometimes with slightly heavier accented drops on beats two and four. One version involves a deeper drop that is accented on the downbeat; this movement has been termed the H.G. Drop, or Holy Ghost Drop, by d. Sabela Grimes, professor of hip-hop at the University of Southern California.

East Coast Stomp

The action in this movement involves the knees, rib cage, and torso. Standing in the same fundamental position as in the drop bounce, pull your left knee upward toward your hips (this action requires hip flexion with a bent knee). Your foot should be flexed and parallel to the ground (see figure 4.5). At the same time, your right leg will bend slightly, and your torso will bend forward from your rib cage. Move your knee and rib cage toward your waist in time with the beat, return to the relaxed beginning position, and then repeat the action on the opposite side.

On the accent of the beat, you should always have one knee in the air at the waistline—not stepping the foot to the floor. In other words, your left knee lifts on count one, your left foot hits the ground on the "and" count, your right knee lifts on count two, and so on. During this movement, your rib cage shifts from side to side to position your weight over the supporting leg.

Figure 4.5 East Coast stomp.

Rock Step

Beginning in fundamental stance, the rock step moves in the opposite direction from the East Coast stomp, with a slight flexion of the left knee on the "and" count and a step on count one. During the leg flexion, the rib cage should curve forward and return to a neutral position with a slight lean back in the left shoulder. The step of the left foot and the lean-back of the shoulders both arrive on the count. This movement continues and repeats on both sides. With each step, the shoulders sway. As the left foot steps, the left shoulder leans back.

ACTIVITY

HUMAN BACKPACK

This move enables you to experiment with weight as a characteristic of hip-hop dance. To try it, seek guidance from your instructor and, if approved, find a partner of comparable size and weight to your own. Stand steady and balanced in fundamental stance with your knees slightly bent and your feet slightly farther than hip-width apart. Next, one dancer hops on the back of the other, and then the standing dancer attempts the drop bounce or the East Coast stomp to feel the weight in the hips. Switch partners, then discuss what you felt during the activity. Be sure that you do this move with the weight toward your pelvis (as if moving to sit on a chair). The weight of the "backpack body" rests on the standing partner's back and pelvis, thus strongly activating the hamstrings, quads, and glutes.

Skipping-Rope Bounce

In fundamental stance, stand with your weight balanced on the balls of your feet. The first step (bounce) lands on count one. The second bounce occurs on the "and" count with an extra lift of the heel; it does not step. Next, shift your weight and step with the other foot on count two. Continue with this pattern while keeping your heels raised slightly off the ground. Your rib cage will shift slightly from side to side in a small lateral rotation.

▶ Rocking

There are three central points in rocking; the neck, the rib cage, and the hips. For each point, the direction in which you rock is based on the direction in which you connect with the beat. If your neck is pulling back to connect with the beat, then your rib cage will project forward. Your hips can either remain neutral or rock back on the beat. Rocking movements of the torso can be either nonfragmented or fragmented.

Nonfragmented Rocking

This type of rocking moves primarily from the hips, usually in a forward motion. It hits the beat at the end of the forward motion before recoiling back to the neutral stance. This rock uses less of the rib cage and neck.

Fragmented Rocking

This type of rocking uses the rib cage, hips, and clavicles (the collarbones, which join the shoulder blades to the breastbone). First, move your rib cage forward and slightly up as your shoulders and hips rock back with minimal movement, ending on count one. Then transition in a downward motion with a slight contraction of the torso just below the sternum or diaphragm area and bend your knees on the "and" count. Finally, push your hips backward, ending on count two. You can do this movement with your feet in parallel position, meaning side by side, or by standing with one foot forward.

ACROSS THE FLOOR

Practicing movements across the floor improves your coordination, spatial awareness, and motor skills. Starting from one corner of the studio space, travel on a diagonal line to the opposite corner with the tempo of the music. Along the way, practice each isolation exercise in counts of four. For example, perform the Pecking, Say What, and Yahmean isolations four times each during one pass across the floor. Once you get to the opposite corner, walk along the short length of the studio to the next corner, then either repeat the same exercises or move on to others in the "tapping the beat" group for the neck. Just because you may focus on one part of the body like the neck, does not mean the rest of the body is stiff. The rest of the body should still groove to the music, but your main focus is on which ever body part you are isolating. This sequence creates a figure eight pattern I call *Sankofa*, from an Adinkra word used by the Akan people of Africa to mean "We must go back and reclaim our past so that it might inform our future journey."

PERFORMANCE DIRECTIONS

Whatever the body's movements, it is useful to articulate the orientation of the body in relation to the space in the room, the person (if any) with whom you are dancing, and the conditions (if such is the case) of dancing in a battle or performing for an audience. In theater, these orientations are referred to as **stage directions** (see figure 4.6); in hip-hop, we refer to this dimension of dancing as spatial awareness.

The basic theater directions for dance are the same as those for any stage performance. The front of the stage (looking out toward the audience) is referred to as *downstage*, and the back of the stage is referred to as *upstage*. The sides of the stage are referred to from the perspective of the performer. In other words, if you are standing on the stage facing an audience, *stage right* is to your right and *stage left* is to your left. Thus when your instructor tells the class to start a movement sequence *stage right*, it means to the right side of the dance space when you are facing the front of the stage.

These directions apply if you are performing hip-hop in a theater space. However, hip-hop dancing is usually performed in a cipher, or circle, in which case the performance space is surrounded by the audience. In this kind of space you can make any direction your "front," and you can face in any direction; sometimes dancers stage a performance to face in different directions. In certain situations, the direction in which you face is determined by external factors. For instance, if you are performing in a choreography showcase, then you face the judges; one the other hand, if you are battling against another crew, then you face that crew.

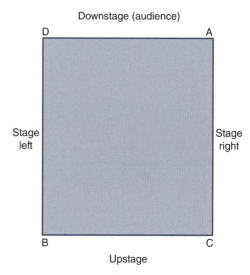

Figure 4.6 Stage directions.

SUMMARY

This chapter has discussed the basics of hip-hop technique. Using the BEATS approach, the chapter has covered alignment, isolations, pulse and groove, bounces, rocking, and ways to create across-the-floor exercises. It has also presented some basic information about performing or battling. These simple movements form the basis of hip-hop dance and will help you achieve the coordination necessary for specific dances presented in the following chapters. Once you become proficient in performing these movements, you will be ready to take on the vocabulary covered in chapter 5.

To find supplementary materials for this chapter, such as learning activities, e-journal assignments, and web links, visit the web resource online.

WEB RESOURCE

Chapter 5

Basic Hip-Hop Dance Steps

Many people perceive hip-hop dance in terms of what is choreographed in today's commercial entertainment world. In reality, choreography is just one aspect of hip-hop, and another main ingredient is social dancing. Hip-hop dances reflect the social dynamics of the times and often respond to pieces of popular music and to pop culture as a whole. In this way, hip-hop dance is like a language: You learn a vocabulary of social dances that teach you how to move your body and give you tools for improvising within the hip-hop aesthetic. You can add these dances to your vocabulary by using what you have learned in chapter 4, especially the four bounces—drop bounce, East Coast stomp, rock step, and skipping-rope bounce.

The dances covered in this chapter span three decades of hip-hop: the 1980s, 1990s, and 2000s. The main focus for learning these movements is to recognize and strengthen your ability to rock, roll (circling), groove and bounce. Whether a dance originated in the 1980s or the current period, learning to see its root structure and how to apply bouncing will help you develop the ability to pick up new dances. This is the key to using what you learn in *Beginning Hip-Hop Dance*. These dances not only root you in the bounces but also help you understand what to do with your arms; how to groove; how to play with timing, levels, and improvisation; and much more. For demonstrations of many of the dances presented in this chapter, visit the web resource.

A great way to warm up is to learn and perform line dances. (*Note:* Dance to the whole song.) These help with building groove, bounce, rolls, rock, two-steps (take a step with the left foot followed by the right foot). Line dances help to build community, trust, and individual expression with your fellow dancers in the space. Line dances usually turn to each direction of the dance space or room, so you build trust that you have someone to watch and learn from, while building individual expression as you find different ways to execute the steps in each sequence of movement. Line dances can be found on YouTube, for example, "Cupid Shuffle" line dance, song by Soldier Boy; "Get It, Baby" line dance, song by Tito Jackson; "Wobble" line dance, song by V.I.C.; "I Want" line dance, song by Chaka Khan; "Uptown Funk" line dance, song by Bruno Mars; "Work" line dance, song by Rihanna; "Fine China" line dance, song by Chris Brown.

DANCES FROM THE 1980S

The rise of danceable rap records from artist like Doug E. Fresh, Heavy D., LL Cool J, Salt 'n' Pepa, Kid 'n Play, and many others created a shift from breaking into a new or different form of hip-hop dancing. As rap music began to take center stage, the advent of music videos help to expose and showcase regional expressions in slang, fashion, hairstyle, music, and dancing. Hip-hop music videos coming out of New York taught the nation and even the world how to do the Running Man, Biz Markie, Happy Feet, and the Steve Martin. In fact hip-hop dances also continued a direct lineage from vernacular or authentic jazz dance, like the 1988 Kid 'n Play Kickstep, which rappers Kid 'n Play originally called the Funky Charleston.

▶ Happy Feet

Happy Feet was a popular dance in New York City clubs in the 1980s. No one is sure who made it up, but it was done when dancers heard "The Show," a song by Doug E. Fresh and the Get Fresh Crew.

Version 1

Begin with your feet hip-width apart and parallel. Face forward with your knees slightly bent and your arms bent at the elbow (between your chest and hips) (*a*). On the "and" count before one, bend your knees slightly and curve forward by relaxing your sternum into a concave position; take care not to exaggerate your shoulder movement. As you bend, put your weight in your right toe and your left heel. On the "one" count, straighten your knees and twist your hips, shoulders, and feet to the left while lifting your right heel and left toe off the ground. As you twist, swing your arms to the right with your left arm crossing slightly in front of your body (*b*). Twist back to the center position with your knees bent, your feet parallel and completely flat on the floor, and your sternum flex (*c*). Now do the same thing but twist right, lifting your left heel and right toe and swinging your arms to the left. Return to a flexed sternum and parallel feet.

Next, pull your hips backward and rock onto your heels, leaving your chest forward as you rock back (*d*). Swing your arms in front of you. Return once more to a flexed sternum and parallel feet, with your hips neutral, before inverting your knees and toes to face inward toward each other as you lift your heels and lengthen your body (*e*). Let your arms pull back. Once you return to a flexed sternum and parallel feet, you can start over (*f*). You can also do this step with a small hop from the central position to all four directions.

Version 2

On "and," begin with your arms down and perpendicular to the floor as you bend your knees (*a*). Swing your arms in a circle to the right (*b*) until they are completely vertical over your head on count one as you stretch your torso upright (*c*). Continue circling back through the low arm position on the "and" count with your chest implode (*d-e*). Keep circling until your arms are parallel to the floor on your right side and your torso is again stretched, this time on the "two" beat. As they reach the parallel position on "two," you should reach the full extent of your twist to the left (*f*). Drop back down to the parallel position on the next "and," with your arms down and your chest flexed. Begin to circle your arms the other way to repeat the entire process to the left as you twist to the right. Your twist to the right will reach its full extent on "four," whereupon you will drop back down on the "and" count, and then you can start again.

a

b

c

d

e

f

▶ The Running Man

This dance became popular after the appearance of the 1987 movie *The Running Man*, starring Arnold Schwarzenegger. The dance is supposed to make it look like you're running in place but with a fun and funky groove; it has spawned many variations. The Running Man is performed in the same way as *Zaouli*, a traditional mask dance of the Gouro, or Kweni, cultures of central Ivory Coast in West Africa.

On "and," lift your right knee and foot and hop backward on your left foot, keeping your weight on the toe and your heel slightly lifted (*a*). (This is a variation of the skipping-rope bounce discussed in chapter 4.) On count one, place your right foot back on the floor in front of you while hopping your left foot backward again, in the same way as before (*b*). As you put your right foot down, transfer your weight onto it in preparation to do the same thing on the other side. Lift your left knee and foot on "and" count as you slide backward on your right foot, then place your left foot in front of you as you scoot back a second time on your right foot (*c*). Repeat.

a

b

c

▶ The Biz Markie

The Biz Markie was created by Marcel Theo Hall, an American rapper whose stage name is the same as that of the dance. It is explained in his 1980s song "Biz Dance." Note that Hall was not a dancer—this is proof that anyone can make up a dance!

Begin in fundamental stance (*a*). In one motion, take a small jump, lifting your torso, and land on your right leg by rolling through your toe, ball, and heel while lifting your left leg with the left knee just above the right. Finish with a slightly bent right knee and your left leg slightly bent and off the floor (*b*). As you jump, wave your left arm upward through your shoulder, elbow, and wrist, ending with the arm slightly bent and extended to your left side (*c-d*). Then pull your left elbow and then your left wrist down to extend your arm across your body toward the opposite hip, shrugging your shoulder up and making a loose fist. As your arm crosses your body, extend your left leg out to your left side (*e*). Repeat on the opposite side, beginning with the jump.

▶ The BK Bounce

The BK Bounce was created by Emilio "Buddha Stretch" Austin. The *BK* stands for Brooklyn, which is Austin's hometown. The step was inspired by another dance called the Steve Martin, which is discussed later in the chapter. Austin was the choreographer for Michael Jackson's "Remember the Time" video, as well as Will Smith's "Men in Black."

Begin in the fundamental stance with your feet parallel and hip-width apart. On the "and" count, lift your heels slightly off the ground and turn them outward slightly, thus turning your toes inward. With your arms bent at a 90-degree angle, lift your elbows up and away from your hips; do not lift them above shoulder height (*a*). On "one," drop your heels and cross your right foot in front of your left foot, bending your knees into a deeper bounce and turning your feet back to a parallel position (*b*). As you drop, pull your forearms back in toward your body, leading with the wrist. On "and," hop into a very small parallel position—smaller than you started in—straightening your knees and lifting your heels. Your elbows will lift outward again (*c*). Then hop again to return to the crossed position with bent knees, bringing your forearms back in (*d*). This step incorporates the skipping-rope bounce, so return to that bounce if you need help getting the groove.

a   b   c   d

▶ The Skate

As its name reflects, the Skate imitates dancing on roller skates. In the 1970s and 1980s, roller skating was very popular in African American communities, and people would dance on their skates. The Skate is also a good transitional movement to sometimes connect dances. The popular Skate dance on the West Coast was completely different from the one on the East Coast. What follows is the East Coast version of the Skate.

Begin in fundamental stance with your feet hip-width apart and parallel. On the "and" count, move your weight onto your right leg as you bend it and lift your left leg (*a*). On "one," step out to the left with your left leg and place it farther than shoulder-width apart from your right leg; as you step out, slightly turn your torso to the right (*b*). Next, transfer your weight onto your left leg and slide your right leg toward your left, then bounce with your legs together by slightly bending your knees and straightening them (*c*). On "and," begin again on the other side. Your arms should be close to you with a loose, relaxed, 90-degree bend at the elbow. Your forearms should be parallel to the floor and hovering between shoulder and hip level, moving along with your steps however you feel they should.

a   b   c

▶ The Steve Martin

The Steve Martin was created by dancer and rapper Steve "Stezo" Williams. As its name suggests, it was inspired by a comedy sketch performed by comedian and actor Steve Martin on *Saturday Night Live*. You can see Stezo perform this dance in the rap group EPMD's music video "You Gots To Chill," where Stezo is the dancer dressed in all yellow. The first dance he does is called the ALF, and the second dance is the Steve Martin.

Begin in fundamental stance (*a*). Lift your heels slightly off the floor (*b*) to prepare the skipping-rope bounce discussed in chapter 4. Each time you drop your heels, rock forward and then back from your rib cage (*c*). Shrug your shoulders so that they lift when you are forward and back but drop when you are in the middle (*d-f*). Now take a step each time you rock, while maintaining the bounce and staying on the balls of the feet. The Steve Martin can also be done in a more advanced way by adding a pivot with a lifted leg to switch directions.

a

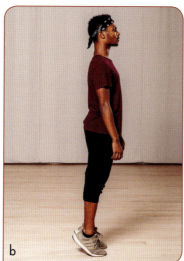
b

c

d

e

f

▶ The Kid 'n Play Kickstep

This dance was invented by dancers and rappers Christopher "Kid" Reid and Christopher "Play" Martin with the help of one of their dancers Nadine "Hi-Hat" Ruffin. The dance was a reinterpretation of the 1920s Charleston, and the duo originally called it the Funky Charleston but renamed it the Kid 'n Play Kickstep and created a song to go with it.

Begin in fundamental stance with lifted heels, preparing to do a skipping-rope bounce with your weight on the ball of your feet. Lift your right foot, keeping your knees together and turning them inward as you lift your left heel slightly (*a*); your right heel should be slightly out to the right side. On count one, take a step forward with your right foot, turning your knees outward with your weight evenly distributed on the toes of both feet (*b*). Repeat on the other side. Then repeat backward, starting by lifting the left foot and then lifting the right. In other words, you should be stepping right, left, left, right. This is a basic Charleston.

To incorporate the Kid 'n Play Kickstep, find a partner and face toward him or her. Both of you will begin on your right leg. Instead of stepping with your left leg, keep it lifted in front of you and click it against the inside of your partner's left foot (*c*), then step backward as you normally would and repeat (*d*).

a

b

c

d

DANCES FROM THE 1990S

In the 1980s, most mainstream hip-hop music came out of New York, and the associated music videos showcased dance moves that were popular in New York City. By the 1990s, however, the West Coast scene and the South were also being heard from, and we began to see more dances that were popular in other places, including California and Atlanta. This section presents a few of those popular dances and the songs they accompanied.

▶ The Bankhead Bounce

The Bankhead Bounce originated on the west side of downtown Atlanta, which was known as Bankhead. It was popularized in 1995 by a song with the same name from rappers L. Atkins and Deongelo "D-Roc" Holmes and by the music video for the song "Benz or Beamer" by Outkast.

Standing in fundamental stance, hold your elbows close to your body and bring your hands to your chest in fists. Lift your shoulders and then drop them, bringing them up and down so that they are down on "one," down on "and," down on "two," and so on. Once you have mastered the bounce in eighth notes, you can begin to play with the placement of your arms as you keep your shoulders bouncing.

The Bart Simpson

The Bart Simpson is another dance from Atlanta. Named after the famous cartoon character, it was inspired by an episode in which the cartoon character introduces a dance called the Bartman. The dance can be seen in the 1992 video "What About Your Friends?" by the R&B group TLC.

Standing in fundamental stance, begin with your torso facing forward. On count one, step to the right with your right foot, bending your knees and turning your hips so that your feet face the right side but your torso remains facing the front (*a*). As you step, swing your arms out so that they are parallel to the floor and out to your left side; they do not have to be fully extended—you can bend them at the elbows and relax a little bit. Both hands should be in fists. On count two, step your left foot into your right and bring your fists back in so that they are in front of your shoulders (*b*). As your left foot touches the floor, lift onto your toes, which should be facing the front (*c*), for a small bounce (*d*). Repeat to the other side, beginning on count three (*e*).

a

b

c

d

e

▶ The A-Town Stomp

As the name suggests, the A-Town Stomp, or ATL Stomp, is another dance that represents the city of Atlanta. It was popularized in hip-hop songs by rappers Young Jeezy and Lil Jon.

Begin in fundamental stance (*a*). On "one," hop once or twice to the right on your left foot (*b*) while kicking your right leg twice by pushing your flexed right heel toward the ground (*c*). The first kick occurs on count one and the second kick on the "and" count. On "two," stomp with both of your feet together (*d*). Repeat on the other side, beginning on count three. Your arms can do whatever you like.

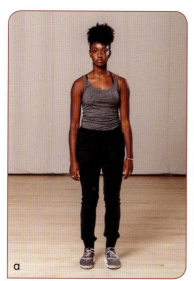

▶ The Humpty Hump

The Humpty Hump, or Humpty Dance, was the creation of rapper Shock G from the hip-hop group Digital Underground. Humpty Hump was the name of Shock G's alter ego, and the dance was a tribute to this persona.

Begin in fundamental stance. On the "and" count before the "one," hop quickly to cross your feet (*a*), then jump them on "one" to a wide stance with your knees bent (*b*). Bounce on counts two, three, and four, hitting the deepest bend on the count as you let your hips move back slightly and then allowing your hips to move forward naturally each time you straighten your knees. You can lean to one side with your torso, and your arms can be outstretched with your hands flexed, windmilling backward one at a time (*c-f*).

▶ The Guess

The Guess is a West Coast dance named after the clothing company. Begin with your feet together and your arms down. On "one," hop to your right with both feet, lifting your arms and landing with your feet angled slightly to the right. Keep your torso facing the front (*a*). On "and," bring your arms down together until they reach waist height (*b*). On "two," bend your knees (keeping them together) so that they are over your toes, following a pathway to the right (*c*). Here, your right arm continues its downward trajectory so that it stretches out and follows the line of your knees diagonally to the right. Your left arm bends as its elbow pulls in the opposite direction. Repeat to the left on count three. Once you are comfortable with the movement, you can play with different arm pathways.

a   b   c

DANCES FROM THE EARLY 2000S

In the early 2000s, the hip-hop social dances were on the rise, and hundreds of new dances were being created throughout the United States. In addition, thanks to the World Wide Web, people no longer had to wait for a music video in order to see the latest dances. Instead, they could see what was happening in real time.

▶ The Jersey Running Man

The Jersey Running Man, officially named the One Leg Get Back, was created by James "Ani" Brown, a teenager in Newark, New Jersey.

In effect, this dance is the Running Man done backward and using the boxer's bounce. Begin with one leg in front of the other and your feet separated about as far as your torso is wide. Your back leg will be the accented leg. Hop your weight onto your front leg on the "and" counts and drop it onto your back leg on counts one, two, three, and four. Again, your elbows are close to your body, bending at a 90-degree angle, and your hands can be closed, crossing and uncrossing with the music however you choose.

▶ Walk It Out

Walk It Out is another dance out of Atlanta. The song of the same name by Unk came out in 2006, but it was the remix featuring Atlanta rapper Andre 3000 from the group Outkast that made both the song and the dance into mainstream hits. This version of the song made the top 10 of the *Billboard* Hot 100 list.

Walk It Out is actually just the Twist. Begin in fundamental stance. Keep your torso facing forward and twist your hips to the right on count one as you step underneath yourself with your right foot. As you twist your hips, your left foot should naturally pivot on the ball of the foot (*a*). On "two," pivot on your right foot and step with your left as you twist your hips to the left. Your heels should stay slightly off the floor the whole time, and your knees should stay bent to make it easier to shift your weight (*b*). Repeat.

▶ The Spongebob

The Spongebob was created in Baltimore, Maryland; it has nothing to do with the cartoon *SpongeBob SquarePants*. The dance was performed with Baltimore club music, which is a type of house music. The most popular songs for the dance were "Tote It" by Rod Lee and "Percolator" by Cajmere.

Begin in fundamental stance. On count one, lift your left leg (*a*) and aim to kick your right buttock with your left heel while hopping on your right leg (*b*). On "and," jump to your left foot, and outstretch your right leg to the right with a flexed foot (*c*). Then repeat by hopping your left leg back in to the center line and bending your right leg to kick your butt. Continue in this manner, hopping out and then back in to your center line. There are no specified arm movements for this dance.

▶ The Wu-Tang

Although it is generally held that the Wu-Tang was created by Glenn Dawson in North Philadelphia, some people have claimed that the dance is from Baltimore. For example, Kenny Thomas, dancer and owner of The Level Dance Complex, has told me that DJs in Philly played Baltimore club music in the 923 Club, which is where the dance was created. The dance was influenced by the Wu-Tang Clan.

Begin in a wide fundamental stance with your knees bent. On the "and" count, lift your arms, bending them at the elbows and keeping the elbows close to your body. Your hands should be closed (*a*). On "one," bring your hands down to about a 90-degree angle, as though you were going to hit your thighs. From there, your arms can do whatever you like as you turn your torso to the right on the "and" count, pivoting your left leg inward and to the right as you lift your left heel (*b*). On "two," return both your torso and your leg to fundamental stance facing the front (*c*). Repeat the whole thing, but this time twist to the left and pivot your right leg.

a

b

c

▶ The Tone Wop

The Tone Wop or Toe Wop is part of a dance movement that emerged out of Harlem, New York. The Tone Wop, along with other dances like the Harlem Shake, Chicken Noodle soup, and Aunt Jackie, is part of Litefeet Nation. A prominent dancer of the Litefeet Nation is Chrybaby Cozie (*cry baby cozie*).

Begin in fundamental stance. On the "and" count before "one," lift your left knee with your left foot underneath the knee in a flexed position (*a*). Place your foot back on the floor with the weight on the ball of the foot (on "one"), then bend your knees into a drop bounce (as described in chapter 4) while turning both your toes and your knees inward so that your lifted heels face out to the sides (on the "and" count) (*b*). Rebound your legs to a parallel position with your feet flat, your weight distributed evenly, and a slight bend in your legs (on count two) (*c*). Repeat the movements on the right side. As your toes and knees turn inward loosely, raise your right arm. As your heels rebound to the parallel position, pull your arm in from the elbow, back to your side. End with a finger snap and repeat on the opposite side.

a

b

c

▶ The Milly Rock

The Milly Rock was created by Brooklyn rapper 2 Milly. The word *Milly* comes from rapper 2 Milly. Milly is short for "militant," in this case meaning stand your ground. After the dance was created, 2 Milly and his crew made it into a song.

Begin in fundamental stance. Keep your elbows fairly close to your body, lifting them to the sides only if necessary, and circle your hands toward your chest as though you were gathering something in (*a-e*). Spread your fingers wide with your palms facing in toward you. Transfer your weight from your right leg to your left leg as you feel necessary, adding slight drops by bending your knees wherever you feel the music should be accented.

a

b

c

d

e

▶ Hit Dem Folks

Hit Dem Folks was created around 2010 at the Booker T. Washington apartments in Columbus, Georgia. The dance places great emphasis on pantomime and includes gestures related to sport actions—for instance, dribbling, crossover, pass and assist, and dunking. The song is danced to "Walked In" by Bankroll Fresh, featuring Travis Porter and Street Money Boochie.

Begin in fundamental stance. There is no one particular way you have to start this dance. The main thing is that you catch the ending dunk pose on the "one" count after two measures of movement improvisation. Basically, count to eight and on the next count ("one") hit dem folks. When you hit dem folks, the ending pose is performed with a slight bounce. One basic example, the hit dem folk pose happens on the cymbal crash in the song "Walked In." Hit the pose on count one, hold for count two, then you can pretend to pass a basketball to the right with both hands (counts 3 and 4), then to the left (counts 5 and 6), then cross your hands one over the other in the middle of your body (count 7), uncross (count 8). Then hit dem folks pose on (count 1) by bringing your left or right arm overhead and the opposite arm across your body chest high as you slightly twist raising one leg with a small lean back in the opposite direction of the lifted leg (leg is bent from the knee). Let all of these motions finish at the same time with a bounce. You can do all kinds of things for counts 3 to 8; let your imagination run wild.

SUMMARY

This chapter has introduced social hip-hop dances from the 1980s, 1990s, and 2000s. Practicing these dances will enable you to become familiar with bounces and grooves and learn how to transition with flow. It will also teach you about arm movements, overall body placement, and more, thus helping you to build your strength and put all of these elements together. When learning more complex steps, always review the basics.

To find supplementary materials for this chapter, such as learning activities, e-journal assignments, and web links, visit the web resource online.

WEB RESOURCE

Chapter 6

History of Hip-Hop Dance

You can connect with dance not only physically—in the studio—but also emotionally and intellectually. The more you know about the history and philosophy of hip-hop dance, the more you can appreciate how this art form integrates mind and body and how it has evolved into the type of dance you are studying today. To help you explore that rich context, this chapter covers key aspects of the history and heritage of hip-hop dance. Specifically, it discusses key retentions in dance practices throughout the African-diaspora and highlights phenomena that helped construct and characterize the movement practices in African American dance communities and the globalization of its aesthetic values.

ORIGINS OF HIP-HOP DANCE

On the surface hip-hop may seem like just another fun dance, but hip-hop is a form of expression and communication that erupted from African American and Latino youth in New York City. Born on the sidewalks and playgrounds of New York City's asphalt jungle, the youthful energy that became known as hip-hop emerged from cultural expressions—ways of communicating through dance, gestures, fashion, talking, and music—as well as sociological phenomena including political abandonment, economic struggle, environmental turmoil, and gang culture. These living conditions can be attributed to high unemployment, exceptionally organized drug distribution, corrupt police departments, and the building of the Cross Bronx Expressway, which led middle- and upper-class residents to migrate north. As a result, between 1973 and 1977, the South Bronx lost 600,000 jobs, more than 5,000 families were displaced, and some 30,000 fires were set in the area, which gave rise to the phrase "The Bronx is burning."

These developments marginalized the African American and Latino communities and left their youth feeling unrepresented and voiceless. In this context, hip-hop gave voice to restless and tumultuous inner-city kids, who also found solace by going down to Manhattan to watch double features of kung fu films. These movies exerted tremendous influence on youth culture in New York, and their concepts mixed with hip-hop culture—in particular the elements of breaking, the creation of new movements, fashion choices, names like DJs calling themselves "Grandmaster" as in Grandmaster Flash, and even approaches to battling. This cultural blend valued strength, skill, style, and discipline, thus creating new values and shaping individual identity among youth. Both regionally and globally, many young people who felt underrepresented began gravitating toward hip-hop philosophies.

Thus the term *hip-hop* encompasses not merely a social dance but an entire subculture, which is based on a particular set of elements, not limited too but including the following:

- Deejays—recorders of time, space, and the sounds and memories of the community
- Emcees (rappers)—storytellers who serve as the voice of the community and reflect its experiences
- Human beatboxers—vocal percussionists who mimic the sounds of the drum machines (beatboxes) used in the early days of hip-hop

DID YOU KNOW?

Part of the deep structure of hip-hop and its combined movement influences can be attributed to the cross-pollination of cultures through the trans-Atlantic slave trade. The slave trade brought European cultures from France, England, Ireland, and Portugal together with at least 14 tribes or nations in Africa, including Sierra Leone, the Bight of Benin, Senegal, Bambio, the Gold Coast, and the Bight of Biafra. They all mixed with the Taino Indians on the Greater and Lesser Antilles, a group of islands located in the Caribbean Sea that includes Cuba, Jamaica, Puerto Rico, Haita, the Dominican Republic, and all of the West Indies. These cultures began to influence each other, whether seriously or for the purposes of satire. Ivan Van Sertima speaks of early travels and an African presence in ancient America in his book, *They Came Before Columbus*. It is possible that cultural influences were happening during these early voyages. In any case, what formed on these islands was eventually brought to North America, and in these deep cultural practices we can find evidence of hip-hop's rich heritage.

- Physical graffiti—the movements and gestures of the dance as informed by people's sociocultural experience, or everyday lived experience (Banes, 1981)
- Writers (graffiti artists)—practitioners of the culture's vivid visual language, which is an improvisational and esoteric style of calligraphy

The deep-rooted structure of hip-hop is found in cultural characteristics of behavior that expand beyond time and geography. These characteristics include individuality, creativity, improvisation, originality, spirituality, stylization, dance posture (bending forward from the waist with the knees bent and the spine slightly curved), vocalization, pantomime, percussion, competition, polyrhythm, and polycentrism. The heritage of hip-hop lives in the social fabric of African and African-diasporic concepts and traditions that include reinventions such as ring shouts, gospel hymns, ragtime, jazz, blues, rock 'n' roll, funk, and soul, all of which culminated in hip-hop.

Ring Shout

Today's practice of the cypher, or circle, is rooted in the **ring shout**, which represents a variety of resilient African musical and dance traits. These traits include spiritual, as well as dance characteristics such as bent knees, curved spine, polyrhythm and polycentrism, improvisation, asymmetrical postures, pantomime, importance to the community, and individuality. These elements recur throughout African American cultural arts and expressions in forms such as the buzzard lope, Juba, blues, ragtime, jazz, rhythm and blues, rock 'n' roll, soul, funk, and hip-hop. They were and still are rooted deeply in African and African-diasporic structures and traditions.

The ring shout has been considered America's first version of choreography. As it developed, the dance was strongly African; it included African rituals and was saturated with African characteristics. It provided a rich and nurturing experience for both enslaved and free blacks and laid the foundation for the black church. The dance served as a prayer or spiritual gathering for enslaved Africans and formed an integral part of their religion and culture. It may have derived from the Yoruba spiritual practice of the **cosmogram**, which was based on the counterclockwise movement of the sun and may have influenced the counterclockwise movement of the ring shout. The circular cosmogram symbol includes a horizontal line through the center to represent the split between humanity and the spirit world. At the same time, the two are connected by a vertical line through the center of the symbol. A circle in the center represents water, which is believed to pass through both worlds.

Cypher

The cypher (also spelled *cipher*) is a central element in hip-hop culture, and its circular shape can be attributed to the circular shape of the cosmogram (see figure 6.1). Members of the community participate in the cypher with the belief that spiritual energy can be transferred in the circular form, which evokes the circle of water within the cosmogram.

The word *cypher* was introduced into the hip-hop lexicon by rappers who followed the teachings of Clarence Edward Smith, better known as Clarence 13X, who left the Nation of Islam to start his own organization, the Nation of Gods and

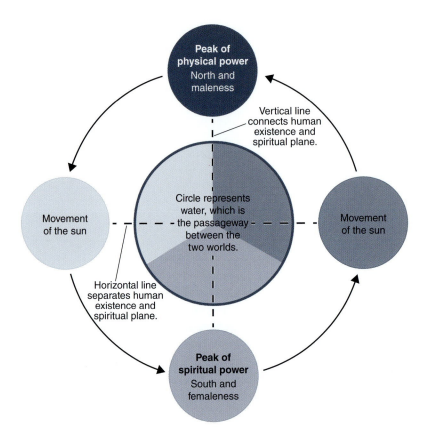

Figure 6.1 The cypher gets its circular shape from the cosmogram.

Earths. This organization is more frequently referred to as the Five Percenters, and it holds that 5 percent of people know and speak truth, 10 percent know truth but conspire to hide it, and 85 percent of people are blind to it. The Five Percenter ideology, known as Supreme Mathematics, includes the following concepts: knowledge, wisdom, understanding, culture/freedom, power/refinement, equality, God, build/destroy, born, and cypher.

The cypher borrows primarily from the first three and last three principles; the idea of being in a cypher is to build through destroying, or to test limits in order to gain strength. Energy is born through a cypher space, allowing ascension to a higher or deeper sense of being. The cypher represents completion, zero, 360 degrees—120 degrees knowledge, 120 degrees wisdom, and 120 degrees understanding—which, together, make up knowledge of self. It is integral to all forms under the hip-hop umbrella. It is a way of engaging in conversation, transmitting ideas, and enabling growth throughout the dance community.

Today, the term *hip-hop dance* includes a myriad of dance forms and styles, such as locking, **popping**, krumping, b-boying, **waacking**, waving, and tutting. However, of all the dance forms associated with hip-hop, only two are in fact hip-hop dances: b-boying and hip-hop party dancing.

▶ B-Boying (Physical Graffiti)

They didn't even have a definite name for the form—they sometimes called it "breaking," but they also referred to it as "rocking down," "b-boy," the "boiyoing," or "just that kind of dancing you do to rap music."

Banes (1994, p. 79)

B-boying was first introduced in the early 1970s as rocking and was danced strictly while standing up, much like Latin dances such as salsa but without the hand-holding in partner dance. In other words, it did not involve spinning with the hands on the ground, which most people associate with breaking. Created in the Latino community, rocking was rooted in various Latin dance forms, such as salsa, rumba, and mambo; it also found inspiration in other dance forms such as tap and authentic jazz. For instance, Willie "Marine Boy" Estrada, a pioneering hustle dancer and rock dancer, once mentioned to me that he used to copy the movements of Fred Astaire and add them to his rock dance.

Rocking

The word *rocking* not only serves as the name of the dance; it also indicates how you do the dance—by rocking, grooving, and swaying. The term *"rockin(g)"* itself was widely used in the 1970s to describe almost anything: You could rock the mic, rock a train with a "piece" (of graffiti), rock the crowd on the "wheels of steel" (turntables), and rock the circle. The term also extended to fashion, as you "rocked" certain articles of clothing, fat laces in your sneakers, your hat, or whatever represented your individual style. In its early days, the dance was referred to as *rocking, boiyoing,* or *going off*. In Brooklyn, it was referred to as *Brooklyn rock* or *freak style*.

According to Trac 2, an early b-boy pioneer, the boiyoing included dances done in the African American community, whereas rock, or rocking, was done in the Latino community in the early 1970s. By late 1974, park jams (outdoor parties in the park) opened up, and African American and Latino communities exchanged dance styles. By 1975, the fusion of top rocking (originally Latino) and floor moves (originally African American) produced a more complete dance form that came to be known as *rocking* and then as *b-boying*. In the 1980s, the dance—referred to as "break dancing" by the media—was extremely commodified, promoted, and exploited by corporate companies for profit. As a result, members of the dance community made efforts to reclaim their art form, which they knew as *rocking* and *b-boying*, to pay homage to the two cultures that had really created the dance.

B-boying, or breaking, is a dance form divided into a few movement practices. For instance, top rocking involves rhythmic upright dancing that introduces a dancer's style and character and is culturally based in Afro-Caribbean heritage. It fuses Latin dances such as mambo, pachanga, rumba, and salsa with authentic jazz dances such as the drop Charleston, the Apple Jack, and mashed potatoes. This movement practice includes drops (stylized ways of getting to the floor) and floor rocking, which has deep roots in Brazilian capoeira (a descendant of Angolan dance).

Floor rocking was influenced by elements from gymnastics and from martial arts films—such as *Disciples of Shaolin* (1975), *Shaolin Temple* (1976), and *36th Chamber of Shaolin* (1978)—which helped breakers develop four devices: strength, skill, creativity, and style. As a result, it created disciplined, flowing moves that displayed rhythm, finesse, and creativity. It also featured "power moves" (displays of strength and balance), "air moves" (acrobatics), and "up-rocking," which, influenced by everyday living and environmental experiences in New York youth culture, used pantomime characteristics as well as gestures found in gang life. Equivalent to the verbal insult tradition known as "the dozens" (or as "mama jokes"), these pantomime movements are called *jerks* and *burns*. A **burn** is a personal improvisational gesture designed to insult one's opponent, whereas a jerk works as part of a four-count step or setup to deliver a burn. In his book *Foundation*, Joe Schloss (2009) suggests that there were three tactics to rocking:

1. Superior dance technique
2. Insulting gestures
3. Mimed physical attacks

There were also three rules of engagement:

1. Understanding the meaning of the gesture
2. Formulating a response
3. Executing without losing the flow of the dance

Finally, there was the "freeze," a metaphoric posture symbolizing a fatal blow delivered to another dancer.

For young people living in devastating circumstances, breaking provided an opportunity to engage with social issues on an abstract level by creating and naming dance moves and choosing their dance names, which helped them establish identities with which to be seen and heard. As graffiti writers, b-boys, deejays, emcees, and so on, young people adopted names such as Method Man, Terrible T-Kid, Mr. Wiggles, Grandmaster, LL Cool J, and Action. These names were labels for real-life personas that liberated individuals from the labels imposed by their environments and their economic status.

> *We transcended, and we became those names, proving to ourselves and the world that we really were and are those personas. . . . We are bigger than life in a context and recognized as cultural superstars by our peers first and the world now . . . making ourselves powerful through a name, an identification that says we are infinitely powerful.*
>
> Sade TCM, graffiti artist, personal communication

The Break and Breaking

In musical terms, the break is the part of a song where an instrumentalist plays an improvised solo; similarly, in dance, the break is a dancer's solo. The term *b-boy*—short for *break-boy*—is credited to **DJ Kool Herc**, a pioneer who is considered the father of hip-hop. In 1970s street lingo, the word *breaking* meant "going off," whether on the dance floor or in an argument. Herc referred to dancers who "went off" to the break of the record as *break-boys* and *break-girls*, or *b-boys* and *b-girls*. The word *break* was also incorporated into the name of some of the early b-boy crews, such as the Breakmasters, Dynamic Breakers, Incredible Breakers, and New York City Breakers. The 1980 hit song "The Breaks," by emcee Kurtis Blow, describes breaks (and brakes) in various ways—for example, "Brakes on a bus, brakes on a car / Breaks to make you a superstar" and "you borrowed money from the mob / And yesterday you lost your job / Well, these are the breaks."

The use of the term *break* is not exclusive to hip-hop. For example, in the 1800s, in buck dancing (an early form of tap dance), a "break" was a drop to the ground. In another example, vernacular jazz dance includes a break step in the shim sham, also known as a T.O.B.A. break (Theater Owners Booking

DJ Kool Herc.

© Joe Conzo Archive 2018

Agency); the shim sham was a stage routine created by Leonard Reed and Willie Bryant circa 1927. There was the Cincinnati Breakdown, a popular social dance of the 1940s. In the Lindy hop, a "breakaway" is a step in which two people separate in order to perform improvised steps before coming back together. In the 1970s, soul dances featured the "backbreaker" (referring to the elasticity of the spine) and the "breakdown" (a side-to-side movement in which the body changed levels as if "breaking down" a little lower). In the 1970s, the average age for a breaker was between 15 and 17; typically, they would stop breaking before the age of 20, because it was considered a dance for young people.

The early 1980s produced two biopic films that gave an accurate presentation of hip-hop culture. *Style Wars* (Silver, Chalfant, & Silver, 1983) profiles New Yorkers who practiced breaking and graffiti art, and *Wild Style* (Ahearn, 1983) is thought of as the first hip-hop motion picture. *Wild Style* features the rappers, deejays, graffiti writers, and breakers from the Bronx who were present for the birth of the hip-hop movement.

Another feature film that came out around the same time is *Flashdance* (Simpson et al., 1983), which, though not generally about breaking, includes one scene focused on members of the Rock Steady Crew. In the scene, this group of breakers and graffiti writers, who were also featured in *Style Wars* and *Wild Style*, display some of their signature moves for nearly a minute and a half. The film grossed more than $200 million at the box office and introduced breaking to the world. As a result, it was no longer just a Bronx or New York dance—now people throughout the world were trying to learn it.

Also in 1983, a West Coast documentary titled *Breakin' and Enterin'* (produced by Topper Carew) introduced pioneers of the street dance culture in Los Angeles and showed the influence of New York breaking on the West Coast dance community.

It also influenced the indie film *Breakin'* (DeBevoise, Zito, & Silberg, 1984), which told the story of a concert jazz dancer who is introduced to the street dance scene. *Breakin'* was less of a biopic and more of a commercialized Hollywood story, and its sequel *Breakin' 2: Electric Boogaloo*, released in the same year, was an even more popular fictional depiction of hip-hop culture.

Another film released in 1984 was *Beat Street*, which was co-produced by Harry Belafonte (Belafonte, Picker, & Lathan). Set in New York, it included many of the original emcees (rappers), deejays, and breakers seen in *Style Wars* and *Wild Style*. It follows two brothers—one a deejay, the other a breaker—as well as a group of their friends, all of whom are invested in hip-hop culture.

By this point, breaking was also being spotlighted on national news shows, talk shows, and advertisements for the likes of Burger King, Levi's, Pepsi-Cola, Coca-Cola, and Panasonic. Indeed, it seemed that everyone was capitalizing on hip-hop, and even the closing ceremonies of the 1984 Summer Olympics in Los Angeles involved 100 breakers. Among the dancers was a young (future Academy Award winner) Cuba Gooding Jr. The heavy exposure of breaking in mainstream media also included TV sitcoms and instructional books and videos complete with manufactured graffiti designed cardboard.

Within the next year, an exploitation of breaking appeared in the film *Cocoon*, directed by Ron Howard (Brown, Zanuck, & Howard, 1985). The film chronicles an elderly group who find they have youthful energy after swimming in a pool occupied

Photo by Eddie Barford/Mirrorpix/Getty Images

Breaking.

by aliens who use the pool to rejuvenate their fellow beings. In one scene, which takes place in a night spot, Art Selwyn (played by seasoned actor Don Ameche) demonstrates his youthfulness by break-dancing in the middle of the club.

This commercialization of breaking began to turn off inner-city youth as companies were in effect trying to sell the culture they had created back to them. However, though hip-hop's first dance seemed to be fading from the spotlight, the music was picking up. The early 1980s saw the release of music from hip-hop artists such as Kurtis Blow, the Sugarhill Gang, and Grandmaster Flash and the Furious Five. Slowly, other groups begin to break into the industry as well, including Whodini (the first hip-hop group to employ dancers as a main feature of their performance), the Beastie Boys, LL Cool J, and Run-D.M.C. By the late 1980s, danceable rap records were being created by emcees such as Kid 'n Play, MC Lyte, Chubb Rock, Doug E. Fresh, Monie Love, Queen Latifah, and Salt 'n' Pepa.

The Golden Era

In the 1980s and early 1990s, California was home to several hip-hop clubs, including Water the Bush (1989-1991), United Nation (1990-1991), and Club Mental (1990-1991). Meanwhile, New York was home to the Roxy (1982-1985), Kilimanjaro, and Rooftop, but the two most popular spots between 1984 and 1987 were Latin Quarters, at 1580 Broadway, and Union Square, at 860 Broadway. Many New York dancers and rappers considered this era and these two clubs to represent the golden age of hip-hop. At that time, the combination of music, dance, people, and violent atmosphere provided an adrenaline rush and energy unsurpassed by other clubs. Eventually, however, that violent atmosphere caused the clubs to be shut down.

> It was an adventure. It was like riding a rollercoaster. . . . It was like jumping out of an airplane. One week you could go to Union Square and see somebody get cut from the forehead down their neck across the back, and the next week, you could see someone get thrown from upstairs to downstairs. And if you made it out of there unscathed, you would come back the next week because the music and the people were so hype.
>
> Emilio "Buddha Stretch" Austin, in the documentary *Wreckin' Shop: Live From Brooklyn* (Martel, 1992)

Hip-hop social dances, sometimes referred to as *party rockin'*, have been present since the beginning of the hip-hop scene in the 1970s. Before breaking—and even during the time when young people had started breaking—there were always social dances. For instance, in the 1979 song "Rapper's Delight" by the Sugarhill Gang, rapper Big Bank Hank mentions three social dances: the freak, the spank, and the bump. Similarly, the 1982 song "Mirda Rock" by Reggie Griffin and Technofunk refers to dancing, rocking, and doing the Smurf—a popular dance of the time, along with others such as the Patty Duke and the Click Clack.

During the 1980s, these social dances took on a flamboyant, b-boyesque battle style while replacing circles of b-boys and b-girls with party rockers. These new hip-hop party dances came into existence because of hip-hop music, as rappers made call-and-

Kid 'n Play doing their signature kickstep.

Photo by Al Pereira/Michael Ochs Archives/Getty Images

response records such as "Woppit" by B-Fats, "PeeWee's Dance" by Joeski Love, and "Do the James" by Super Lover Cee and Casanova Rud. As rap music continued to take center stage, the advent of music videos helped to showcase various regional and communal expressions in slang, fashion, musical background, and dance. Popular dances included the Steve Martin and the Biz Markie in New York City, the Bart Simpson and the Bankhead Bounce in Atlanta, and, in California, the Guess and the Dee-Daa, an extremely advanced dance that is difficult to do correctly.

Hip-hop social dance also continued a direct lineage from vernacular jazz movements in dances such as (in the 1980s) the Kid 'n Play Kickstep (originally called the Funky Charleston) and (in the 2000s) the Spongebob, which is the reverse of the scissor-kick Charleston of the 1930s. It also included a continuation of animal dances stemming from the African tradition; for instance, ragtime and early jazz dance had the Grizzly Bear and the Buzzard Lope, and hip-hop had the Snake and the Chicken Head. Hip-hop even used inspiration from television, movies, and toys to create new, more advanced dances, such as the ALF, the Running Man, and the Cabbage Patch.

By the mid-1990s, hip-hop music had shifted, and the music videos featured fewer dancers and crews from the community. Instead, this era saw the rise of video vixens—that is, female models who appeared in hip-hop-oriented videos and were portrayed (or fetishized) as fragile or submissive. This approach used fewer social dances but more precise movements similar to those used in standard cheerleading formations, such as the Bowling Pin, Diamond, Diagonals, Windows, and Squares. This type of presentation would become known as *commercial hip-hop*, and it tried to assimilate hip-hop fashion, style, and attitude. It was sharp but void of individual personality.

APPROPRIATION AND APPROXIMATION OF HIP-HOP

Hip-hop dance classes feature many different titles and descriptors. Here are a few: **West Coast style**, **Los Angeles style**, commercial, and new style (not to mention the craziest one I've heard: Pussy Cat Dolls in Heels Hip-Hop). None of these terms and titles reflect true hip-hop dance culture. Instead, they are names associated with the commercial dance scene and may have been created in order to promote studio classes. As a result, they have no defined style, technique, or foundation; they are simply hybrids of choreography based on lyrical, concert jazz, and ballet motifs promoted as hip-hop. Here is a brief explanation of these dance classes.

West Coast Style

West Coast style, a name that is interchangble with Los Angeles style (details below), came not from the hip-hop dance community but from studio dance culture. In fact, this label is common language amongst the studio trained dancers who are doing a hybrid ballet, jazz motif that is not reflective of some of California's pioneers, such as Scheme Team, Soul Brothers, and other popular crews from African American communities up and down California's coast.

Los Angeles Style

Los Angeles style, or *LA style,* as it is often known, was popularized in music videos and stage shows; it pulls from both street dance and concert jazz. For example, Omar Lopez, who was a member of the New York group Shades with Randy Connor and Keith Williams, began dancing with Janet Jackson and, along with Williams, brought the group's fusion of street styles such as hip-hop, house, and vogue. They also incorporated some influence from Jackson's and Paula Abdul's movements, such as the long clean lines of concert jazz. Their style of dance made an influential addition to Jackson's stage choreography.

Commercial Hip-Hop

Commercial in this case does not stand as a prefix for *hip-hop*, which would suggest that commercial is a style of dance. Rather, the name has become a popular marketing term for studio classes, which again involves a hybrid of choreographic styles. However, hip-hop dance itself, as a form, does not change. Think about it this way: Ballet in a movie is still ballet, not "movie ballet" or "commercial ballet," and the same goes for hip-hop dance. The venue may change, but—whether it appears on stage, in a movie, in a studio, or in a club—authentic hip-hop is still hip-hop.

Thus what we see now in the mainstream is not an evolution of hip-hop as much as it is an approximation of the movement and a commercialization of its aesthetic. Hip-hop dance in the deep structure has not changed; the expressions born in the African, Latin, and American communities are still present today. Authentic hip-hop can be found in wards in the South and in Harlem, North Philadelphia, the Bay Area, South Central (i.e., South Los Angeles), and the South Side of Chicago. Hip-hop's concept of freestyle has influenced many dancers performing today who have studied the concert jazz stylings of Bob Rizzo, Gus Giordano, Matt Mattox, Bob Fosse, and Eugene "Luigi" Facciuto, as well as more current jazz and contemporary dancers such as Mia Michaels and Brian Friedman. These dancers use

Broadway jazz movements and techniques, and they appropriate Vogue culture, movement, and gestures, sprinkled with hip-hop attitude and movements, as they apply a circle mentality of freestyle. Direct, strong, and aggressive, it is a beautiful presentation—but it is not hip-hop dance.

New Style

New style, correctly spelled **nu style** in the hip-hop world, is short for "New York style," much like *Nuyorican* means "New York Puerto Rican." The term comes from the influence exerted by dancers in the New York scene on people in other parts of the world—particularly France and Japan. Many dancers in these countries appreciate the style of dancers in New York and refer to their style as *nu style*.

During the late 1980s, rappers hired their friends or popular dancers in their communities for their groups or performances. In New York City, for example, there were Scoob and Scrap, who performed with rapper Big Daddy Kane; TCF (The Chosen Few), with Kool G Rap and DJ Polo; the IBM dancers, with the rap duo Nice & Smooth; the Invincible, with Kid 'n Play; and the Boyz, with Heavy D. In California, dance teams included the Soul Brothers, with emcee Def Jeff, and the Scheme Team, with Divine Styler, among many others. Other crews and dancers freelanced for various artists. Examples include Leslie "Big Lez" Segar, Marjory Smarth, Jossie Thacker, Rosie Perez, Nadine "Hi-Hat" Ruffin, Fatima Robinson, the Mystidious Misfits (who can be seen in the video "Toss It Up" by Zhigge), the IOU dancers (in the 1988 Kid 'n Play video "Gittin' Funky"), the MOP-TOP crew (in the 1989 Doug E. Fresh video "Summertime"), and the Gucci Girls (in the 1988 video "Groove Me" by the R&B group Guy).

These dancers and community crews gave birth to the social dance style of the 1980s and 1990s, creating dances and influencing fashion as well as hairstyles. These influences led to an international community of hip-hop dance practitioners.

COMMERCIALIZATION OF HIP-HOP DANCE

The appropriation and assimilation of hip-hop dance in the late 1990s produced what became known as *commercial hip-hop*. Of course, the use of hip-hop music does not always result in the creation of authentic hip-hop dance. In fact, most of what has been popularized in the mainstream media as hip-hop dance today is not true hip-hop. Mainstream notions of hip-hop dance are typically characterized by the showcased choreography featured in movies such as *Step Up* (2006) and its sequels, in television shows such as *So You Think You Can Dance*, and in competitions such as Hip Hop International. Though commercially successful and entertaining, these productions do not give completely accurate representations of the underground hip-hop dance community.

Also in the 1990s, hip-hop dancing in music videos and stage performances reflected a shift from community dancers to studio-trained dancers. This change resulted from many factors, including the production of less danceable rap records and the aging out of established dancers, who went off to college or started families.

For instance, in the 1988 music video "Jam Jam (If You Can)" by the R&B group The Gyrlz, you can see dancers Stretch, Tron, and Link from the crew **Elite Force** (then known as MOP-TOP) doing hip-hop social dances such as the Gucci, the Steve Martin, Roger Rabbit, ALF, the Running Man, and others. By the mid 1990s, their choreography had evolved, but it retained the true hip-hop dance aesthetic in their freestyle approach, which used various forms under the hip-hop umbrella: locking (discussed in chapter 7), b-boying, party dances, house dance, popping (discussed in chapter 7), and other sub styles related to popping, such as waving, tutting, and ticking.

For example, in the music video "Men in Black," choreographed by Stretch, you see the foundational hip-hop bounce and groove with modified use of popping and locking, as well as reinterpretations of 1980s social dances such as the Guess and the Skate. This style was an Elite Force trademark, and, with lead choreography from Stretch, their work—with Michael Jackson (in "Remember the Time"), Layla Hathaway, Da Brat, and Mariah Carey—kept true hip-hop alive in the "commercial" arena. Overall, the choreography used by Elite Force blended hip-hop, popping, breaking, locking, and house dance—or what they called *hip-hop freestyle*.

As the term *hip-hop* became more of a marketing tool, many pop artists claimed to be doing "hip-hop," and many dance studios began offering commercial hip-hop classes. In these classes, studio-trained jazz dancers used techniques from ballet, modern dance, and Broadway and Hollywood jazz to create choreography, then labeled it "hip-hop" without substantive consideration of the aesthetic values, history, techniques, or foundation embedded in the community that created the movement.

In this way, hip-hop has become a tangible commodity of an intangible cultural heritage. As scholar Tricia Rose has noted, "For many cultural critics, once a black cultural practice takes a prominent place inside the commodity system, it is no longer considered a black practice—it is instead a 'popular' practice whose black cultural priorities and distinctively black approaches are either taken for granted as a 'point of origin' . . . [or] isolated 'technique,' or rendered invisible" (Rose, 1994, p. 83). It is this exact approach in teaching that presents hip-hop dance as an arbitrary movement, thus negating the social values, principles, and techniques that are culturally significant to its meanings and purpose.

In the 1990s, countless pop singers and groups—such as Justin Timberlake, NSYNC, Usher, R. Kelly, Jennifer Lopez, Beyoncé, Janet Jackson, and Britney Spears—relied heavily on choreography based on a hybrid of dance styles labeled as "hip-hop." At the same time, you could still see authentic social hip-hop dances coming out of the South, such as the Bankhead Bounce, the Bart Simpson, and the A-Town Stomp. It wasn't until 2001, however, that hip-hop social and party dances experienced a resurgence thanks to multiple artists, who featured social hip-hop dancers and dances in their videos. For instance, rapper Eve's music video "Who's That Girl" featured Harlem dancers doing the Shake, also known as the Harlem Shake. Around the same time, young dancers from Harlem were also featured doing the Shake in the G Dep music video "Let's Get It" (featuring Black Rob and

P. Diddy). And in 2003, the Nelly song "Shake Ya Tailfeather" and the Chingy song "Right Thurr" both featured the St. Louis dance known as the Monastery (also known as the Chicken Head).

The fact that hip-hop dance has gone mainstream is exciting. These expressions of hip-hop are embedded in and reflective of the African American community, and they shine light on those who have gone unsung. As stated by Halifu Osumare in her book, *The Africanist Aesthetic in Global Hip-Hop: Power Moves*, "That this aesthetic has now been globalized does not detract from its Africanist origins; it only further humanizes and universalizes the African cultural foundation." (2007, p. 60)

SUMMARY

Hip-hop brings together culturally diverse people better than any other dance form. Hip-hop dances are created from people's social environments and their lived experiences and common gestural practices. They also incorporate influences from popular culture in the form of sayings, music, movies, and so on—all of which help create the ongoing hip-hop aesthetic. These social dances feature multiple rhythms with movements that generate and expand from multiple center points.

As new forms and styles are born, they continue to illuminate personal and cultural dynamics of ethnicity and diversity and to recall the history, heritage, and stories of the African American people who created these American art forms. These expressions were and still are being created and developed by marginalized adolescents in black and brown communities, and these dances have empowered generations of people who felt, or feel, powerless. Through hip-hop dance, you can honor and understand the art form and the people who have shed blood, sweat, tears, and years. They spoke through the dance and showed the world that they and we matter, and that people have a voice regardless of social class or cultural ideology.

To find supplementary materials for this chapter, such as learning activities, e-journal assignments, and web links, visit the web resource online.

Chapter 7

Hip-Hop Dance Forms

Hip-hop dance is one of the most popular and most misunderstood forms of cultural expression in the world. Similar to authentic jazz, also known as vernacular jazz, hip-hop is a way to express concerns, frustrations, aggressions, ideals, and exuberance. As a result, the outlet of music and dance can help a person maintain balance and peace while dealing with day-to-day life experiences. Indeed, this is a way in which African American people have expressed themselves since 1619.

In order to understand these forms of expression, you must understand the significance of cultural identity in the dance forms and lineages that have been placed under the abstract umbrella we now refer to as *hip-hop dance*. Though the term has aided in communication with and unification of people from many cultures, it has also caused confusion on a global scale. For instance, some believe that the hip-hop foundation includes popping and locking while forgetting the party dances expressed in, through, and because of rap and hip-hop music; in fact, popping and locking, are **funk-styles** placed under the umbrella term.

Thus the biggest problem with the umbrella term is that it fails to identify the people who created or innovated the other forms. For instance, even though b-boying was hip-hop's first dance, it can also be viewed as a funk dance; it was danced primarily to funk music and named after the breaks in funk music and other types of records. In fact, there were no hip-hop records at that time, and the term *hip-hop* was first used to define records in 1979 and to define the culture in 1981. Similarly, the reason that 1980s party dances are referred to as *hip-hop dance* rather than as *breaking* is that they were danced to music classified as hip-hop. In addition, not everyone is aware that the term *hip-hop* serves a dual purpose, naming both the culture and the particular dance form (party dances).

A detailed historical perspective has been provided in chapter 6. In turn, this chapter covers some of the dancers and crews who pioneered these art forms and examines how they saw the body as a tool of expression. Like all artists, these figures in hip-hop dance history were influenced by the society in which they lived. The rest of this chapter, then, provides some key information about the people, crews, and forms that live under the umbrella term—the people who created or pioneered the dances, the places in which they were developed, the terminology and vocabulary used to talk about them, the differences in technique, and the histories.

▶ LOCKING

Locking, or, as it was first named, *Campbellocking*, was created by **Don "Campbellock" Campbell**. Born in St. Louis in 1951, Campbell was raised in Los Angeles, where he grew up with a love for art. After sketching throughout his teenage years, he attended Los Angeles Trade–Technical College to study commercial art. During his time there, he was influenced by local dancers Sam Washington, Dozer Ray, and Sweet Tee. Although Campbell was a shy person—and not a dancer—he was encouraged by Washington to begin learning and doing the popular dances of the time. As he imitated what he saw Washington doing, he accidentally created what would become a worldwide dance phenomenon.

Although most people feel that Campbell's creation was influenced by the Funky Chicken, the real influence was the Robot Shuffle, which was a popular dance at the time. The Robot Shuffle is a type of two-step in which the dancer steps sideways with the left leg and slides the right leg over and slightly behind the left as the arms sort of sway in the same motion. Specifically, as the left leg steps left, the arms come toward the middle of the body; then, as the right leg slides behind the left, the arms sway to that side of the body. These actions are then repeated on the other side. As Don Campbell attempted the fluid movements of the dance, he locked his arm joints on a downward motion on each side, thus creating a stop at the end of the movement.

The movement was christened in Campbell's name thanks to the 1970s practice of addressing a person by last name. Thus Sam Washington said, "Hey Campbell, do that lock!" and in the spring of 1970 the dance received its name: The Campbellock. After that, Campbell himself became known as Campbellock.

Over time, Campbell inadvertently began to create a vocabulary for his movement style. For example, when people laughed at him, he would point at them; thus pointing became part of the vocabulary. Another example was related in a story told by dancer Jimmy "Scoo B Doo" Foster about a move that Campbell created called Give Yourself Five. As Foster explains, when giving other dancers five, Don had a heavy hand, and when he gave you five, you really felt his power. Giving someone five is a sign of acknowledgment, so if there wasn't anyone around to give him five, Campbell would give himself five. Thus this move also became part of his movement language.

In addition, Campbell said that whatever he was doing, people would start clapping. Even if it was wrong, people clapped, so he kept doing it. For example, he would play hambone—that is, create body percussion by slapping the thighs, hands, chest, and so on—and the audience would give positive feedback. Consequentially, hambone became part of his locking style and ultimately part of the dance. Hambone, which is part of the cultural heritage of African American music and dance, is also known by other names, such as playing the bones, playing the spoons, and patt clap Juba.

The Campbellock Dancers

Campbell became a local celebrity and influenced imitators as he won countless dance contests. He showcased locking while dancing with Damita Jo Freeman on the brand-new nationally syndicated television show *Soul Train* in 1971. The show also featured other local dancers from the community, such as Jimmy "Scoo B Doo" Foster, Pat Davis, Tyrone Proctor, Charles "Robot" Washington, and Fawn Quinones. However, six months into the show's second season, Campbell suggested that the dancers be paid and began to protest the unfair wages (a soda and a box of chicken); in response, he was kicked off of the show.

With the advice from Toni Basil, he took his dismissal as a cue to start his own group. He gathered dancers whom he thought performed his dance the best and who were also part of the Soul Train Gang—for example, Fred "Penguin" Berry, Greg "Campbellock Jr." Pope (who received his moniker from Damita Jo Freeman because he imitated Campbell so well), Leo "Fluky Luke" Williamson, Bill "Slim the Robot" Williams, and Adolfo "Shabba-Doo" Quinones. At one point, Basil took on the role of manager. She was not a dancer on *Soul Train* but had sought out Campbell in order to learn the dance. Hailing from a performing family, Basil was a well-known dancer and choreographer at the time. She had worked on shows such as *Shindig!* and on the movie *T.A.M.I.* (Teen Age Music International) *Show* in the 1960s, and she played a major role in arranging television appearances for Campbell's group and contributed to its choreography. Fred Berry would eventually leave the group to star in the television sitcom *What's Happening!!* under the nickname Rerun, and the group chose Tony "GoGo" Lewis Foster as an alternate.

Originally known as the Campbellock Dancers, the group appeared on television shows such as *The Tonight Show, The Carol Burnett Show, The Dick Van Dyke Show,* and *In Concert*. They were also the first nonmusical group to perform on *Saturday Night Live*. In addition, the group toured as an opening act for Frank Sinatra, performing at Carnegie Hall and Radio City Music Hall, and also appeared at Disneyland, the

Hollywood Bowl, and the Playboy Club. They were the only "street" dance group to present an award (as themselves) at the Grammy Awards ceremony. Campbell even recorded his own record, "Do the Campbellock," whereupon, due to legal reasons, he changed the name of the group to The Lockers. In addition, the group was depicted in animated form in the film *Hey Good Lookin,'* which was shot in 1976 but released in 1982. Written, directed, and produced by Ralph Bakshi, the film featured Don as Boogaloo Jones, the leader of a gang called the Chaplains that battles a rival gang known as the Stompers.

Thus the Lockers were a huge success, achieving the American dream. Don's personal vindication came when he and the group returned to dance on *Soul Train*— not as part of the Soul Train Gang but as paid special-guest performers. In 1976, Basil left the group, after which she went on to record her hit song "Mickey." After the group disbanded in 1977, Shabba-Doo starred in the 1984 film *Breakin'* and its follow up, *Breakin' 2: Electric Boogaloo.* Don continued dancing with his group, bringing in new members to replace those who left and thus generating new energy.

Locking in Pop Culture

Campbell's influence has continued to be felt from the 1970s to the present day. In 1977, for example, *Saturday Night Fever*, one of the biggest hit movies of the decade, featured a young John Travolta as Tony Manero, a charismatic paint-store clerk looking to make it big. In the iconic disco scene, Travolta's character demonstrates his superiority on the dance floor through locking. Travolta, who practiced for months, trained with Denis George Mahan, aka Deney Terrio, who was a member of Don Campbell's second locking group (that group also included Bill "Slim" Williams from the original group, as well as newcomers Lionel "Big D" Douglass, Alfa Anderson, Lewis "Deputy" Green, Tony "GoGo" Lewis, and Stan "The Man" Rodarte, to mention a few). Most people mistake the key movement performed by Travolta as disco or hustle, but in fact it is a stylized, choreographed movement drawn from locking.

Similarly, in 1984, locking was one of the dance forms featured in the movie *Breakin'*, which starred Shabba-Doo. And throughout the 1990s, pop sensation Mariah Carey employed a group of dancers, known as Elite Force, who specialized in "street" dance styles such as locking, hip-hop, popping, and house. Elite Force and friends can been seen using locking movements in Carey's music videos, television appearances, and tours.

Among other examples, pop singer Usher's concert training coach and dancer-choreographer, Jerry "Flo Master" Randolph, was trained by Greg "Campbellock Jr." Pope and supplied locking movements for Usher to perform. Janet Jackson also used locking in her Rhythm Nation World Tour 1990 and in her music video "Alright," both of which featured choreography from Anthony "Bam Bam" Thomas. In 2001, Brian "Footwork" Green used locking when he choreographed the Mýa's music video "Free," for which he won an American Choreography Award for outstanding achievement in a hip-hop music video.

Today, locking is considered one of the dance forms to learn under the umbrella of hip-hop and is a global phenomenon taught and performed worldwide. Campbell himself still teaches and judges locking competitions, serving for example as one of the main judges for Hip Hop International (a competition created by Howard Swartz, who also created the hit TV show *America's Best Dance Crew*). Thus Campbell's dance continues to inspire people to get up and dance—or, as Don might say, to "shake it and lock it."

▶ WAACKING

Waacking originated in the 1970s in the gay club scene in Los Angeles. According to original *Soul Train* dancer Tyrone Proctor, waacking was first called *posing*, because the dancers would stop and pose. Later, it became known as *punking*, based on a derogatory term for gay men. The term was coined as an inside joke amongst the gay dancers by DJ Michael-Angelo who was the main DJ at the gay club Gino. One favorite song to waack to was "Papa Was a Rolling Stone" by The Temptations; the dancers would pose to the rhythmic patterns of the bass guitar.

The original posers were greatly influenced by motion pictures, silent films, musicals, and, more specifically, such stars as Marilyn Monroe, Fred Astaire, Greta Garbo, and Charlie Chaplin. The first posers included Arthur Goff, Tinker Toy, Andrew Frank, and Lamont Peterson, who was a dancer on *Soul Train* and one of the first to incorporate shoulder and then full arm movements into posing. Tyrone Proctor and Toni Basil from The Lockers said that Peterson was one of the first dancers to leave California for New York, where he and New York dancer Mickey Lord pollinated the dance style.

The dance was popularized in the heterosexual dance community through both *Soul Train* and a friendly dance battle between Tinker of the Outrageous Waackers and Shabba-Doo from The Lockers. Playful blends emerged as the two copied each other and added locking textures to waacking. Thus Shabba-Doo, the first heterosexual male to learn the dance from the original posers, made it "cool" for other heterosexual males to do the dance.

In a YouTube clip, Kumari Suraj explains the origins of the term *waacking*: stating that, "the original *Batman* series which used onomatopoeias in fight scenes—'pow,' 'punch,' 'bang,' 'crash,' is where you get the name for the movement 'whack,' which means 'to strike with force.' But whack was a verb/action for one movement, not the name for the entire style that the punks were doing."

After his days on *Soul Train*, Proctor moved from Philadelphia to California in 1972 and then to New York City to join the group Breed of Motion, which included legendary waacker and voguer Archie Burnett and legendary voguer Willi Ninja. The dance style known as **vogue** gained mainstream exposure and popularity when Madonna featured voguers in the music video for her 1990 hit song "Vogue." The dance developed in the gay ballroom club scene in New York City and then spread to major cities throughout the United States and around the world.

Proctor has suggested that in its early stages vogue was more statuesque, focusing on presentation, and later dance performance in drag balls. The first queer masquerade ball had taken place in Harlem's Hamilton Lodge back in 1869, and ball events were also hosted in Webster Hall's East 11th Street building in the 1920s (Valenti, 1988). In his 1940 book *The Big Sea*, Harlem Renaissance luminary Langston Hughes described drag balls as "spectacles of color" (Hughes, p. 273). In March 1953, *Ebony* magazine stated more than 3,000 contestants and spectators gathered in Harlem's Rockland Palace, "to watch the men who like to dress in women's clothing parade before judges in the world's most unusual fashion shows."

The vogue dance style is characterized by model-like poses and influenced by the angular, linear, and fixed body postures featured in *Vogue* magazine, which is where the dance gets its name. Proctor believes that the form didn't take off as a complete style of dance until after the appearance of waacking. Before Willi Ninja created his legendary House of Ninja, Breed of Motion exerted a huge influence on dance in New York City and in Japan. Suraj suggested that the group's influence in New York City led to a tendency for waacking and vogue to resemble each other.

In the 1980s, Shabba-Doo and other dancers, such as Ana "Lollipop" Sanchez, helped to keep waacking alive by performing it on the variety television series *The Big Show* and in the 1984 films *Breakin'* and *Breakin' 2: Electric Boogaloo*. Sanchez would later appear in jazz artist Herb Albert's 1991 music video "North on South Street,"

© TheBlackSheep Photography/Luis Rocha dos Reis

which shows multiple street dancers performing hip-hop and house dances and Sanchez doing a waacking solo. From the late 1980s to the mid-1990s, waacking was in danger of dying out, and its resurgence in the late 1990s was sparked by dancer Brian "Footwork" Green's monthly dance event known as the House Dance Conference. Since then—thanks to YouTube, dance events such as Street Start in Sweden, and the efforts of key individuals (such as Green, Proctor, Suraj, Burnett, and Samara "Princess Lockeroo" Cohen)—waacking has become one of the fastest-spreading dance styles since the explosion of b-boying in the 1980s. Indeed, it has developed worldwide appeal.

Waacker and voguer, Archie Burnett.

▶ ELECTRIC BOOGALOOS AND POPPING

Popping and **boogaloo** are two forms created by Sam "Boogaloo Sam" Solomon, who was born in Fresno, California, in 1957. As a young kid, Sam would dance socially with his family and draw inspiration from cartoons. He learned the term *boogaloo* from his grandparents as one that referred to doing eccentric or unconventional movements with one's neck, feet, hips, and torso. *Boogaloo*, or *bugalú*, refers to a form of music as well as a form of dance—not a specific style of dance but an expression of free-spirited movement.

It has been suggested that the word *boogaloo* is derived from the word *boogie*, which comes from *mbugi*, a word from Kikongo (one of the Bantu languages) that means "devilishly good" (Ventura, 1985; Thompson, 1983). As a music form, boogie-woogie was a style of piano playing first made popular as ragtime in the late 1800s. In turn, "the rhythmic aspects of ragtime derived from the banjo dance-tune style which was related to Patting Juba" (Hitchcock, 1969, p. 122). The percussive style of Juba is found in the Jola people of Senegal; the Juba style of music making is the same as that described in regard to locking. *Boogie* may also relate to the phrase *boogie woogie*, which was popular during the Harlem Renaissance in the 1920s and 1930s. *Boogie woogie* derives from a Bantu term *mbuki-mvuki*, meaning "to take off in dance performance." Other possible connections include the word *bugs* (with the *u* pronounced as an "ohhh" sound) from the Mandé people of West Africa—meaning "to beat drums"—and the word *bogi* from Sierra Leone, which means "to dance."

In the 1950s and 1960s, particularly among African Americans and Latinos, the popular musical genres for dancing were rock 'n' roll and jump blues; in addition, the Latino boogaloo was on the rise, but no specific dance was attached to that music. Popular songs that mentioned African American boogaloo dance included Don Gardner's "My Baby Likes to Boogaloo," Wilson Pickett's "Boogaloo Down Broadway," and James Brown's version of the 1962 Chris Kenner song "Land of a Thousand Dances" (which mentions 16 popular dances). In Brown's version, titled "There Was a Time," he sings about the dances he used to do, one of which was the boogaloo. The only similarity between these dances and Sam Solomon's boogaloo lay in the fact that they were improvised.

During his teenage years, Sam began to take his dancing a little more seriously, and he teamed up with childhood friend Nate "Slide" Johnson. The two were influenced by Robert Shields, a street performer in San Francisco who was influenced by toys and went from doing mime to perfecting a robot technique that profoundly affected Sam and Nate, as well as the future hip-hop dance community. Shields teamed up with Lorene Yarnell to create the comedy act known as Shields and Yarnell. They specialized in taking on robot personae, and in 1977 they were featured in their own comedy-variety program on television.

Meanwhile, Sam teamed up with Nate Johnson and another friend, Joe "Slim" Thomas, as well as two other dancers—Darnell "Twist-O-Flex Don" McDowell and William Green, known together as the Ace Tre Lockers—to form a group called the Electronic Boogaloo Lockers. Joe and Nate did the Robot, Darnell and William performed locking movements, and Sam did his boogaloo, which consisted of fluid body rolls of the neck, torso, hips, and knees. Mixing the boogaloo with popping created the unique style in Sam's form. This is not to be confused with the Robot or other forms—such as bopping, Filmore, strutting, and tutting—that were created by other dancers in different parts of California, such as the Bay Area.

Popping, which gets its name from the sound that Sam used to make when he was dancing, consists of repeated muscle contractions in the neck, biceps, triceps, and chest, along with a snapping of the legs for full-body pop. In 1978, Sam's younger brother, Timothy "Popping Pete" Solomon, began learning the dance, and he eventually became a member of the group. This early group would go on to appear on such shows as *Kicks* and *The Midnight Special* (an American late-night musical variety program that aired on NBC as a regular series from 1973 to 1981), and *Soul Train* (the first nationally syndicated, black-owned program featuring music and dance). *Soul Train* was created and owned by Don Cornelius, who also served as the first host of the program, which lasted for 35 seasons.

Now living in Long Beach, California, Sam brought in new members: Gary "Scare-crow Scally" Allen, Dane "Robot Dane" Parker, Cedric "Creep'n Sid" Williams, and Marvin "Puppet Boozer" Boozer. The crew got its first big break in performing with American dancer and choreographer Jeff Kutash, who served as director for the late Michael Jackson's This Is It tour. During their time with Kutash, the group's named was shortened from the Electronic Boogaloo Lockers to the Electric Boogaloos.

In 1979, when the group was asked to perform on *Soul Train*, member Cedric "Creep'n Sid Williams performed a move known as a backslide. A year earlier, Michael Jackson had seen it performed by *Soul Train* dancer Jeffrey Daniel. Known to most people as the moonwalk, the move goes in a forward motion and panto-mimes a person walking on the moon; however, *backslide* is the correct name of the move, which goes backward in a sliding manner. In 1982, after Michael Jackson learned the move from Daniel and friend Jerome "Casper" Canidate, he made the step famous for the second time during his performance on the Motown 25 awards show. The move is originally a tap step known as the Get Off—a novelty step used by tap dancers to exit the stage at the end of a solo; its creation is credited to tap dancer Bill Bailey, who can be seen performing it in the 1943 movie musicals *Cabin in the Sky* and *Stormy Weather*.

In 1981, Boogaloo Sam's cousin Steven "Skeeter Rabbit" Nichols joined the group, and during this decade members of the group began working with Michael Jackson. Jackson always kept an eye out for the latest dances coming out of the African American community. In the 1970s, he had incorporated locking movements into his performances, and in the 1980s, he was profoundly influenced by popping and boogaloo style. In fact, he hired dancer Bruno "Pop N Taco" Falcon to train him in the style for 15 years.

Jackson also used members of the Electric Boogaloos in a few of his music videos. For instance, Popping Pete and Robot Dane appeared in the video for "Beat It." Another member, Steve "Suga Pop" da Silva, appeared in the videos for "Beat

It" and "Thriller." Suga Pop, also a member of New York City Rock Steady Crew, joined the Electric Boogaloos in 1997, along with Pop N Taco and Steffan "Mr. Wiggles" Clemente. Members of the Electric Boogaloos also appeared in Jackson's *Ghosts* and *Captain EO* projects, including Hugo "Mista Smooth" Huizar, Jazzy J, and Donald from the Boo-Yaa T.R.I.B.E. Members of the Electric Boogaloos have gone on to perform with Usher, Chris Brown, Janet Jackson, Justin Timberlake, Madonna, Missy Elliott, and other artists. The Electric Boogaloos continue to tour the world—teaching, performing, and judging.

Emilio "Buddha Stretch" Austin

Emilio "Buddha Stretch" Austin, or Stretch, as he is commonly known, was born and raised in Brooklyn. Stretch, as well as other dancers who danced at the famous Latin Quarters and Union Square night clubs, have been credited with fusing old-school dance (dance forms that became popular in the 1970s, such as locking, top-rocking, waving, and popping) with new-school dance (hip-hop party dances and house dance of the 80s and 90s). This blending created what is known today as *freestyle hip-hop*, which came into existence sometime in the mid to late 90s.

The commercial explosion of breaking culture in the mainstream media reached its peak in the form of commercials, books, videos, and the release of such films as *Flashdance*, *Breakin'*, *Breakin' 2: Electric Boogaloo*, and *Beat Street*. As mentioned in chapter 6, this heavy exposure led to what felt like a lack of concern for the essence of the culture. However, with the advent of danceable rap records, a new style of dancing was being created, and Stretch was at the forefront.

Stretch along with friends Peter Paul, Tron Warren, Giuliano Lincoln Wells, and Danilo Ignacio Sobers, collectively known as the JAC dancers, which stood for (Just Another Crew or Jack of All Crafts), began performing weekly at the Union Square nightclub Latin Quarter nightclub in New York City. Stretch was chosen as the group's choreographer, and JAC began opening up for rap groups such as BDP (Boogie Down Productions), Heavy D, Salt 'n' Pepa, and DJ Jazzy Jeff and Will "The Fresh Prince" Smith. In 1987, Stretch was hired to dance with Whodini, the first rap group to employ dancers as part of its stage performance, which inspired other rap groups to follow suit (see chapter 6).

In 1991, Stretch and his friends created a crew called MOP-TOP, which stands for "motivated on precision toward outstanding performance." The new crew continued performing for many of the hottest rap and R&B acts in the 1990s and were featured in the PBS documentary *Wreckin' Shop: Live from Brooklyn* (Martel, 1992). The original members of MOP-TOP were Austin, Ejoe Wilson, Henry "Link" McMillan, and Caleaf "Big Leaf" Sellers; the extended membership included Peter Paul Scott, Jamel "Loose Joint" Brown, Jemel "Rubber Band" Boatwright, Tony Davila, Casper, Ade, and Ramier Sellers. MOP-TOP also included the Mystidious Misfitss, or Misfitss for short, Kito Portee, Marquest Washington, Massiah "Peek-a-boo" Hill, and Stephen "Prance Lo" Corbie. These dancers all played a major role in the hip-hop party-dance scene and appeared in countless music videos and concerts that influenced dance in the United States and around the world and all members credit Stretch as their teacher or major influence.

Stretch went on to become the choreographer for Mariah Carey for most of the 1990s. During that time, he also choreographed for multiple recording artists on the national and international levels. For instance, his work can be seen in the 1990s Will Smith hits "Miami," "Gettin' Jiggy Wit It," and "Men in Black," all of Mariah Carey's videos, Wyclef Jean's "We Trying to Stay Alive," as well as Michael Jackson's "Remember the Time." It was on the set of this Jackson video that the crew officially became known as Elite Force, reflecting their desire to be a force to reckon with. The crew's dancing is rooted in African American values, such as exhibition of cool; ideals of style; and use of multiple rhythms, musical awareness, gestures, attitude, fashion, spirituality, and individuality. They have helped shape the global landscape of hip-hop dance and continue to teach, perform, and judge competitions around the world.

Soul Brothers

The Soul Brothers are a West Coast hip-hop crew out of Los Angeles who are well-known for their battling skills. The crew was founded in 1986 by Daddy around the time of the Trendy era, a style of party dances popular in Los Angeles area.

The Soul Brothers began working in the industry during hip-hop's golden era (1989-1991), and at that time the crew consisted of Kraig E., V-Love, and Legendary. They brought a style of dance that differed from the New York style. They didn't just use the dances created in New York. They used the popular dance steps created in Los Angeles; their choice of movement in relationship with the music though funky and groovy presented, at times, to be more sporadic. They performed with rapper Jeffrey "Def Jef" Fortson and appeared on many television shows, most notably *Soul Train* and the variety show *In Living Color*. They also choreographed for the R&B group BBD (Bell Biv Devoe), which developed from the famous group New Edition. Even as they enjoyed success with industry artists and showed the influence of their mentors—The Lockers—the Soul Brothers still performed their own shows.

Other dancers and crews were also instrumental in the development and popularity of hip-hop dance. For instance, Scoop and Scrap Lover danced for rapper Big Daddy Kane; before that, they belonged to the IOU Dancers, who did the first group choreography for a hip-hop artist, in the Salt 'n' Pepa music video "Tramp." In other examples, China and Jette were known for dancing with De La Soul. Stezo and Fendi danced for EPMD, and Stezo went on to record hit song "My Turn." UTFO members Doc Ice and Kangol Kid started off as dancers for rap duo Whodini before creating their own rap careers. Stretch and Cliff Love began dancing for Whodini after UTFO next. The Mystidious Misfits were featured in Zhigge's video "Toss It Up." Here are some additional examples: IBM dancers E-Boogie, Mike Swift, Cornbread, Cliff Love, and Showtime danced for the rap duo Nice & Smooth, and Safari Sisters Alison and Kika danced for rapper Queen Latifah. Leg One and Leg Two danced for MC Lyte; G-Wiz and T-Roy danced for Heavy D; and Damn Hype danced for Jazzy Jeff and The Fresh Prince. Thick and Thin danced for Steady B. Selema, and Shane danced for Sweet T. The hip-hop crew known as the Scheme Team danced for Divine Styler, and Geronimo danced for LONS (Leaders of the New School). TCF's (The Chosen Few's) Shawn and Kenny danced for Kool G. Rap and DJ Polo. Chris "Shaik" Mathis danced with the R&B group Guy, and Kiam and Shane danced with rapper Slick Rick.

▶ HOUSE

House music is a genre associated with gay subcultures in the 1970s; it first became popular in the nightclubs in New York City, New Jersey, Baltimore, Philadelphia, Washington, D.C., Detroit, and Chicago. The name comes from a popular club that was the genre's birthplace in the warehouse district of Chicago in 1977. The Warehouse club was patronized primarily by gay African American and Latino men and operated under the direction of Robert Williams, who hired New York DJ Frankie Knuckles to spin at the club. Knuckles' unique blends led to the selling of Warehouse mix tapes; as people shortened the name from *Warehouse* to *house*, the genre's name was set.

The sound that gave birth to house music also gave birth to disco, and it can be credited to one man—drummer Earl Young. Young was the lead drummer for the soul group The Trammps out of Philadelphia and played lead drums for many groups that recorded in that city. His distinctive style led him to speed up the beat on a recording for the R&B and soul group Harold Melvin and the Blue Notes, which featured Teddy Pendergrass. The song in question was "The Lost I Lost," a ballad that Young thought was too slow. In response, he played a 4/4 beat on the kick drum and eighth notes on the snare, which, combined with his extensive use of the hi-hat cymbals, created a new sound. Thus, in 1973, "The Lost I Lost" would be considered the first disco record, and this sound provided the backbeat for what became known as house music.

In the late 1980s, hip-hop clubs such as Union Square and the Latin Quarters—two of the best clubs for hip-hop music and dance—closed, due to violent atmospheres. The advent of **hip-house** came when dancers began to venture out to house clubs and hip-hop dancers began the transition from hip-hop to full-blown house.

Marjory "The Lotus" Smarth

Hip-hop artists were beginning to rhyme over house tracks, which created a new genre of music that was called *hip-house* by artists such as Fast Eddie, in Chicago, where the style is said to have originated. Others included Tyree Cooper and Doug Lazy, from Washington, D.C. The style gained mass appeal through the New York rap group Jungle Brothers' hit song "I'll House You." It was produced by New York house music producer Todd Terry, who also produced the smash hit "It Takes Two" by Rob Base and DJ EZ Rock.

Big Daddy Kane released two hip-house records: "The House That Cee Built" and "Another Victory," which used Booker T. and the M.G.s' beat from "The Melting Pot," a classic R&B and funk record that was popular in the early house clubs.

Kane, considered one of the best emcees at the time, may have connected with a harder hip-hop audience than that of Rob Base, who had a more commercial appeal, and the Jungle Brothers, who were more Afrocentric in their visual and musical approach. In this context, the song "Wiggle It," by the hip-house duo 2 in a Room, peaked at number one on the U.S. dance chart, and the video featured Marjory "The Lotus" Smarth.

Smarth, a member of Dance Fusion (a pioneering New York hip-hop and house crew), played a major role in introducing hip-hop dancers to the house dance scene. During an interview I conducted with her on our way to the Bust a Move hip-hop dance event in Montreal, she shared with me the following perspective: "As the hip-hop dancers began going to clubs that played house music, they brought with them their hip-hop attitude and dance vocabulary, changing the dynamics of the hip-hop steps to fit the faster BPMs [beats per minute] of house music." Some hip-hop steps were simply done faster but had the same name. Others received new names. According to Tony "Sekou" Williams, a hip-hop and house dancer and member of Dance Fusion (a pioneering dance crew in New York City), "Hip-hop steps like the Criss-Cross and Roger Rabbit just became faster, but the Happy Feet became the Gallop and the East Coast stomp became the Farmer." The Farmer is a fundamental step in house dance and received its name from the coveralls that were in fashion at the time.

Such steps would become staples of house dance, and, when mixed with the many movements used in house clubs, led to the creation of such steps as the Salsa Hop, Loose Legs, and Scribble Foot. The early house-club generations did not have a truly codified vocabulary for individual steps, but the elder generations would tease and influence the hip-hoppers—or, as some elders called them, *clubheads* or *grasshoppers*. The elders included people such as Louis Kee, Frankie Thomas, Mia Phillips, Kahim Johnson, Robert "Pee-Wee" Mickens, and Voodoo Ray, who were some of the first to make the transition from hip-hop to house.

DID YOU KNOW?

Many dancers wore white sneakers so that others could see their feet amid the dark and the flashing lights of the club. Some also used baby powder on hardwood floors to make it easier to spin and dance in circles.

In New York, the question of what is or is not house dance is the subject of a fervent history of contention between the earlier generations of dancers, who frequented New York City house clubs and parties, and the dancers of the hip-hop generations, who would codify house dance steps in the 1990s. The New York clubs of the 1970s and early 1980s included David Mancuso's Loft, as well as the Paradise Garage and Bonds International, for the underground scene; the Saint, mostly for white gay men; Studio 54, for the mainstream crowd; and the Fun House, for Puerto Ricans. For both generations, house was and is a spiritual vibe.

Founded on freestyle dance and personal expression, these clubs provided spaces open to all movements and body types, where people could freely experience and express the moods of the music. For many, they also provided a safe haven from social inequalities. You would find all types of dancing bodies and forms of dance, from free movers to those engaging in jazz, modern, ballet, b-boying, African, salsa, tap, and other forms.

The presence of hip-hop dancers in house clubs after the closure of the hip-hop clubs is shown in two documentaries, *House of Tres* (1990) and *Wreckin' Shop: Live From Brooklyn* (1992). *House of Tres* is mostly about house music and vogue but also shows hip-hop party dances, b-boy up-rocking movements, and some house dance. *Wreckin' Shop,* which featured the pioneering hip-hop crews MOP-TOP and the Mystidious Misfits, showed both hip-hop and house dance. In fact, because the show did not differentiate between the two, dancers in California thought they were seeing a new blend.

Wreckin' Shop also made MOP-TOP a favorite dance crew in Japan. They were invited to visit that country in 1994, and Ejoe Wilson from MOP-TOP claims to be the first person to teach house dance there. House has since become a global phenomenon, continuing the traditions of individuality and spirituality and the essence of love personified that one feels in a house club.

> *We are people who thrive in the other eight hours of the day, the flip side of your 9-to-5, the nightlife. We are one nation underground, hiding in plain sight. We are eight million stories told through sound, motion and flashing lights, rhythmic nomads who wandered the land of a thousand dances and called it Eden, a religion by accident, conceived in the black, Latino and queer communities that gave birth to the Gallery, the Loft and the Paradise Garage.*
>
> Brian Polite, house dancer/poet

SUMMARY

The dance forms discussed in this chapter are now most often categorized under the umbrella of hip-hop. Additional styles and forms associated with hip-hop include tutting, waving, toy man, puppet, animation, jookin', tuffing, strobing, ticking, sac-ing, strutting, litefeet, bone breaking, Chicago footwork, and krumping.

Hip-hop culture has now gone mainstream; it has brought more culturally diverse people together than anything else in the world. Hip-hop speaks through dance and shows the world that people can have a voice regardless of class or cultural ideology. It values the individual but also uplifts the community. As new styles are born and continue to illuminate personal and cultural dynamics of race and diversity, let us not forget about the lineage—the stories and the people that have created these art forms.

These expressions are largely, but not only, created by youth of African-diasporic descent. The art form has empowered generations who felt or feel powerless; these marginalized adolescents have created the art form and given it an identity. They have invented and named movements and given them value, purpose, and intention.

They have developed techniques that are continuously shared and learned around the world. Let's appreciate how these art forms build community, and let's honor the people who shed blood, sweat, tears, and years. They are part of American history.

Hip-hop is for everyone. It is not something you do; it is something you live. It doesn't care about your political, economic, or religious background. Hip-hop only cares about one thing: Can you rock? Can you rock the mic, the turntables, the wall, or the dance floor? It's about empowerment, conviction, and intention.

I leave you with my definition of the word DANCE. D- stands for discovering the A- autobiographical self, to N- negotiate, C- creativity, and E- express. I wish you all the best on your journey. Now go and express yourself and know that your feelings, your ideals, your dance, your body, and your expressions are valuable. They matter. I leave you with the Yoruba word *Ase* (pronounced ah-shay), which denotes power, command, and authority—the ability to manifest words into reality and produce change.

> To find supplementary materials for this chapter, such as learning activities, e-journal assignments, and web links, visit the web resource online.
>
>

GLOSSARY

abduction—Action characterized by moving away from the body's midline.

adduction—Action characterized by moving toward the body's midline.

African-diasporic—Related to the dispersion of people around the world from the African continent.

alignment—Positioning of the body for proper performance; specifically, arrangement of the skeletal system to line up the bones in a way that transfers weight through the center of each involved joint.

anatomical position—Erect standing position with the feet forward, the arms down by the sides, and the palms facing forward with the thumbs outward and the fingers extended.

anterior—Involving the front of the body or of a body part.

appendicular skeleton—Portion of the skeleton that includes the bones of the limbs. The pectoral girdle consists of the clavicle and scapula, while the pelvic girdle consists of the hip bones, sacrum, and coccyx.

attitude—Body position implying an action or mental state; for our purposes here, emotional quality of music as displayed through the body.

axial skeleton—Portion of the skeleton that includes the bones of the skull, vertebral column, sternum, and ribs.

b-boying—Dynamic form of dance, also known as *breaking*, that was created by African American and Puerto Rican people in New York City and is set to hip-hop, funk, or breakbeat music.

boogaloo—Term that may have roots in the Bantu language (with a meaning of "devilishly good") and has carried various meanings in music and dance, including the following: musical genre created by teenage Cubans and Puerto Ricans that was popular in the United States in the 1960s; way to say "get down" and "enjoy yourself" during the Harlem Renaissance; and style of music pioneered by Boogaloo Sam that consisted of fluid body rolls of the neck, torso, hips, and knees.

bouncing—Foundational type of movement in hip-hop dance, which is characterized by a buoyant quality in both movements and transitions.

break—The part of a song where an instrumentalist plays an improvised solo; similarly, in dance, the break is a dancer's solo.

breaking—See entry for *b-boying*.

burn—Personal improvisational gesture that is designed to insult an opponent and is performed in partnership with a *jerk* as part of a four-count step or setup to deliver the burn.

call-and-response—African-diasporic tradition rooted in African cultures, often exemplified in church services ("Can I get an Amen?" "Amen!"), and used in dance when the music calls for a response in the form of a particular dance or movement.

cancellous tissue—Spongy form of bone tissue.

canon—In dance, the creation of overlapping imitations by initiating the same sequence at different times.

cartilaginous joint—Joint connected by cartilage.

circumduction—Movement that travels in a complete circle.

commercial—Term used to describe not a technique or type of dance but a dance performance displayed in venues concerned with or engaged in commerce (such as advertising or selling products).

compact tissue—Bone tissue that forms the rigid section of the organ and the bone cell within it.

concentric muscle contraction—Shortening of a muscle that results in visible joint movement.

cosmogram—One of many symbols from African Kongo or Bakongo culture used by African-diasporic people.

counterflow isolation—Movement in which the neck is isolated by moving in one direction while the torso moves in the opposite direction.

counterrotation—Movement in which the upper and lower parts of the body go in opposite directions.

cypher—Practice (similar to a ring shout) in which people gather in a circle and use rap or dance to display skill in a friendly, sometimes aggressive manner.

DJ Kool Herc—Pioneer DJ who helped develop hip-hop music and culture.

Don "Campbellock" Campbell—Dancer and choreographer who created locking.

drop—Stylized way to get to the floor when breaking or b-boying.

dynamic (isotonic) muscle contraction—Contraction that changes the length of the involved muscle.

eccentric muscle contraction—Contraction that involves lengthening the muscle.

Elite Force—Pioneering hip-hop dance crew from Brooklyn who have choreographed and danced in the entertainment industry since the mid-1980s.

extension—Increase in the angle of a joint.

fibrous joint—Joint held tightly together so that little or no true movement exists in it.

FITT principle—Acronym referring to frequency, intensity, time, and type of activity performed.

flexibility—Ability of a joint to move freely through the full range of motion.

flexion—Decrease in the angle of a joint.

fluid body—Consistent body movement that is free of jerking or stopping.

fundamental—The necessary base or core principles essential for developing in the movement.

funk-styles—A term coined by Timothy "Popping Pete" Solomon to cover the forms and style performed by West Coast Poppers and Lockers to deter people from putting multiple dance forms under one title and to create conversations that differentiated the techniques, forms, vocabulary, and pioneers in each form.

grooving—Moving smoothly with the tempo of the music.

hip-house—Musical genre that mixes elements of house music with hip-hop.

hyperextension—Extension past the natural position, as when bending far backward.

isolation—Movement performed with some parts of the body while keeping other parts still.

kinesthetic awareness—Ability to put together experience and sensory input to guide one's body in movement, thus enabling both imitation of movements seen and creation of movements based on one's imagination.

lateral—Involving the parts of the body that are farthest from the midline.

ligament—Tissue that attaches bone to other bone.

locking—Form of dance, created by Don Campbell, that combines the fluid movements of social dance of the 1970s with short stops or pauses.

Los Angeles style—A loaded phrase; there are a few ways to understanding this term. One way is that what is known as Los Angeles style was actually inspired by three dancers from New York called Shades. These dancers moved to Los Angeles and began working with Janet Jackson; their approach to choreography was based on multiple dance forms included New York hip-hop and house. Another way to view this phrase is the dance style of young dancers in the Los Angeles "street" dance scene, which was very abstract, flows, and ground movements. And third is the sharp, gestural movement in popular in North Hollywood dance studios.

macronutrient—Chemical elements that provide essential fuel for the body and are found in food in the form of carbohydrate, protein, and fat.

medial—Involving the parts of the body closest to the midline.

muscular endurance—Ability of a muscle to apply continual force.

muscular strength—Maximal capacity of a muscle to exert force against a resistance.

musicality—Generally, understanding of music; in dance, understanding of how a given movement relates to the music.

nu style—Shortened term for "New York style"; used in reference to hip-hop dances and culture in New York City.

personal space—Space in which one can engage in leg, arm, and body extensions either while standing in place or while moving around without invading a neighbor's space.

polycentric—Using more than one center of movement in the body.

polyrhythmic—Using two or more rhythms simultaneously; in dance, movement of two or more body parts to different rhythms.

popping—Form of dance performed by consistently contracting one's muscles (specifically, the sterno-cleidomastoid muscles in the neck, the pectorals, the biceps, and the triceps) to the tempo of the beat.

posterior—Involving the back of the body or of a part of the body.

PRICED—Acronym that refers to an injury-healing method focused on protection, rest, ice, compression, elevation, and diagnosis.

prone position—Position characterized by lying facedown.

repertoire—Collection of dances, movements, or pieces that an individual or company is prepared to perform.

ring shout—Transcendent religious ritual first practiced by enslaved Africans in the West Indies and North America.

rocking—Style of dance (specifically, a part of b-boying) that involves rocking motions such as top rocking (performed while standing) and floor rocking (performed on the ground).

rotation—Turning of the anterior surface of a muscle either inward or outward.

routine—Series of sequences that form a cohesive dance.

sequence—Particular order of movements or dance steps.

shin splints—Condition characterized by tenderness or other discomfort on the front of the shin, especially when jumping.

space—Position that a dancer must maintain within a group, which requires an understanding of personal space as it relates to general space.

spatial awareness—Understanding of how one's body is oriented in space and how the parts of one's body are positioned with respect to both the dance space and other people.

sprain—Injury that involves the tearing of a ligament or other joint tissue.

sprung floor—Floor that aids performance by absorbing shock, thus allowing a softer feel when landing jumps or rolling or spinning on the floor.

stage directions—Direction's used by actors, dancers, choreographers, directors, and designers to identify locations on the stage (for example, *upstage, downstage, stage left, stage right*).

strain—Injury that involves overstretching and tearing of a muscle or tendon fiber.

subchondral tissue—Smooth tissue found at the ends of bones and covered by cartilage.

supine position—Position characterized by lying face-up.

synovial joint—Type of joint that allows the most freedom of movement and is the most common type.

tendon—Tissue that attaches muscle to bone.

time—In dance, time signature or meter signature; also, notational system used in Western music to specify number of beats per measure.

tone—Character of a musical or vocal sound determined by its pitch, quality, and strength.

visualization—Type of affirmation that involves envisioning oneself doing or completing a movement or choreography.

vogue—A modern American dance form created in the African American and Latino LGBTQ community, with origins dating back to the early 1900s in Harlem.

waacking—Form of dance, also known as *punking*, created in the LGBT clubs of Los Angeles during the 1970s disco era.

West Coast style—See *Los Angeles style*.

REFERENCES

Ahearn, Charlie (Producer & director). (1983). *Wild style* [Motion picture]. United States: Submarine Entertainment.

Banes, Sally. (1981, April 22). Physical graffiti: Breaking is hard to do. *The Village Voice*, 31-33.

Banes, Sally. (1994). *Writing dancing in the age of postmodernism.* Middletown, CT: Wesleyan University Press.

Belafonte, Harry (Producer), Picker, David V. (Producer), & Lathan, Stan (Director). (1984). *Beat street* [Motion picture]. United States: Orion Pictures.

Blow, Kurtis, Ford, Robert, Jr., Moore, James B., Simmons, Russell, & Smith, Larry. (1980). The breaks [Recorded by Kurtis Blow]. On *Kurtis Blow* [album]. Chicago: Mercury Records.

Brown, David (Producer), Zanuck, Richard D. (Producer), & Howard, Ron (Director). (1985). *Cocoon* [Motion picture]. United States: 20th Century Fox.

Clippinger, Karen. (2016). *Dance anatomy and kinesiology.* 2nd ed. Champaign, IL: Human Kinetics.

DeBevoise, Allen (Producer), Zito, David (Producer), & Silberg, Joel (Director). (1984). *Breakin'* [Motion picture]. United States: Cannon.

Dunford, M. (Ed.) (2006). *Sports nutrition: A practice manual for professionals.* 5th ed. Chicago: American Dietetic Association.

"Female Impersonators: Men Who Like to Dress Like Women Combine Fantastic Fashion Shows with Gay Masquerade Balls in New York and Chicago," *Ebony*, March 1953, 64.

Glass, Barbara. (2007). *African American dance: An illustrated history.* Jefferson, NC: McFarland.

Hitchcock, H. Wiley. (1969). *Music in the United States: A historical introduction.* Upper Saddle River, NJ: Prentice-Hall.

Hughes, Langston. (1940). *The big sea.* New York: A.A. Knopf.

Malone, Jacqui. (1996). *Stepping on the blues: The visible rhythms of African American dance.* Urbana, IL: University of Illinois Press.

Mannes, Elena. (2011). *The power of music: Pioneering discoveries in the new science of song.* New York, NY: Walker.

Martel, Diane (Director). (1992). Wreckin' shop: Live from Brooklyn [Television series episode]. In Mindy Goldberg (Producer), *Alive TV.* PBS.

National Strength and Conditioning Association, Earle, Roger W., & Baechle, Thomas R. (2003). *NSCA's essentials of personal training.* Champaign, IL: Human Kinetics.

Osumare, Halifu. (2007). *The Africanist aesthetic in global hip-hop: Power moves.* New York, NY: Palgrave Macmillan.

Roholt, Tiger C. (2014). *Groove: A phenomenology of rhythmic nuance.* New York, NY: Bloomsbury.

Schloss, Joseph. (2009). *Foundation: B-boys, b-girls, and hip-hop culture in New York.* New York, NY: Oxford University Press.

Silver, Tony (Producer), Chalfant, Henry (Producer), & Silver, Tony (Director). (1983). *Style wars* [Motion picture]. United States: Plexifilm.

Simpson, Don (Producer), Bruckheimer, Jerry (Producer), & Lyne, Adrian (Director). (1983). *Flashdance* [Motion picture]. United States: Paramount Pictures.

Thompson, Robert Farris. (1983). *Flash of the spirit: African and Afro-American art and philosophy.* New York, NY: Random House.

Valenti, Chi Chi. (1988). Nations. *Details*, 158-74.

Ventura, Michael. (1985). *Shadow dancing in the USA.* Los Angeles: Jeremy P. Tarcher.

SUGGESTED RESOURCES

Change, Jeff. (2005). *Can't stop won't stop: A history of the hip hop generation.* New York, NY: St. Martin's Press.

Charnas, Dan. (2010). *The big payback: The history of the business of hip hop.* New York, NY: Penguin.

Chernoff, John Miller. (1979). *African rhythm and African sensibility: Aesthetics and social action in African musical idioms.* Chicago, IL: University of Chicago Press.

Damasio, Antonio. (1999). *The feeling of what happens: Body and emotion in the making of consciousness.* New York, NY: Houghton Mifflin Harcourt.

DeFrantz, Tomas. (2002). *Dancing many drums: Excavations in African American dance.* Madison, WI: University of Wisconsin Press.

Dixon Gottschild, Brenda. (2003). *The black dancing body: A geography from coon to cool.* New York, NY: Palgrave Macmillan.

Gaunt, Kyra D. (2006). *The games black girls play: Learning the ropes from double-dutch to hip-hop.* New York, NY: New York University Press.

George, Nelson, with Banes, Sally, Flinker, Susan, & Romanowski, Patty. (1985). *Fresh: Hip hop don't stop.* New York, NY: Random House.

Homans, Jennifer. (2010). *Apollo's Angels: A history of Ballet.* New York, NY: Random House.

Huntington, Carla Stalling. (2007). *Hip hop dance: Meanings and messages.* Jefferson, NC: McFarland.

Jourdain, Robert. (1997). *Music, the brain, and ecstasy: How music captures our imagination.* New York, NY: Morrow.

Leland, John. (2004). *Hip: The history.* New York, NY: HarperCollins.

Myss, Caroline. (1996). *Anatomy of the spirit: The seven stages of power and healing.* New York, NY: Three Rivers Press.

Noland, Carrie, & Ness, Sally Ann. (2008). *Migrations of gesture.* Minneapolis, MN: University of Minnesota Press.

Roberts, John. (1995). *From hucklebuck to hip-hop: Social dance in the African American community in Philadelphia.* Philadelphia, PA: Odunde.

INDEX

Note: Page numbers followed by *f* or *ff* indicate that a figure or multiple figures will be found on those pages.

A

abdominal isolation 44-45
across the floor movements 48
aesthetic 37
African-diasporic dance forms 2
alignment and stance 39, 39*f*
amygdala 41*f*
anatomical position 26, 26*f*
anatomy 22-25, 23*f*, 24*f*, 25*f*
ankle sprains 28
appendicular skeleton 22
A-Town Stomp, the 63
attitude 16, 37
auditory cortex 41*f*
Austin, Emilio "Buddha Stretch" 57, 95-96
axial skeleton 22

B

Bankhead Bounce, the 61
Bart Simpson, the 62
Basil, Toni 89
b-boyesque battle style 81-82
beatboxers, human 74
BEATS approach 36-39
Beat Street (movie) 80
Biz Markie, the 56
BK Bounce, the 57
Blow, Kurtis 79
body percussion 89
bones, make-up of 23-24
boogie woogie 93
bounces 8
bouncing in dance 46-48, 47*f*
brain processes while dancing 41*f*
break and breaking
    commercialization of 81
    described 2-3, 78-79
breakaway 79
Breakin' and Enterin' (documentary) 79-80
Breakin' (movie) 80
buck dancing 79
burn, definition of 78

C

call-and-response style 36, 81-82
calligraphy 75
Campbellock Dancers 89-90
Campbellocking 88
Campbell, Don "Campbellock" 88
cancellous tissue 24
carbohydrate 32
carrying dance gear 15

cartilaginous joints 23
cerebellum 41*f*
Charleston. *See* the Kid 'N Play Kickstep
choreo. *See* commercial hip-hop
choreography
    America's first version of 75
    based on hip-hop 85
    in movies 84
Clarence 13X. *See* Smith, Clarence Edward
classes. *See* dance classes
clubheads 98
Cocoon (movie) 80
commercial hip-hop 4, 83
commercialization of breaking 81
commercialization of hip-hop dance 84-86
communication
    hip-hops concepts of 5
    nonverbal 3
compact tissue 24
concentric muscle contraction 25, 25*f*
connective tissue 26
cool-down 11
cosmogram 75
counterflow isolations 45-46
cypher
    described 5
    history of 75-76

D

dance bags 15
dance classes
    dressing for 13-14
    environment 4
    gear for 15
    mental preparation 16-17
    performance evaluation 7
    physical preparation 17-18
    student expectations and role 5-6, 6-7
    structure of 8-11
    teacher's role 4-5
    titles of 83-84
Dance Fusion 98
dance gear, carrying 15
dances from the 1980s
    Biz Markie 56
    BK Bounce 57
    Happy Feet 52-54
    Running Man 55
    Skate 58
dances from the 1990s
    A-town Stomp 63
    Bankhead Bounce 61

dances from the 1990s *(continued)*
  Bart Simpson 62
  Guess 65
  Humpty Hump 64
dances from the 2000s
  Hit Dem Folks 71
  Jersey Running Man 66
  Milly Rock 70
  Spongebob 67
  Tone Wop 69
  Walk It Out 66
  Wu-Tang 68
Dawson, Glenn 68
deejays 3, 74
diaphragm isolation 44, 44*f*
dietary fat 33
DJ Kool Herc 78-79
dressing for class 13-14
dynamic muscle contractions 24-25, 25*f*

E

East coast stomp 46, 47*f*
eccentric muscle contraction 25, 25*f*
electric boogaloos and popping 93-95
emcees (rappers) 3, 74
endurance, muscular strength and 17
etiquette, student 6-7

F

fat, dietary 33
fibrous joints 22-23
fitness, principles of 31-32
FITT principle 31
Five Percenters 75-76
Flashdance (movie) 79
flexibility, stretching for 17-18
flooring 20-21, 20*f*
floor movements and exercises 10
floor rocking 78
Foster, Jimmy "Scoo B Doo" 89
Foundation (Schloss) 78
fragmented rocking 48
freestyle 85
freeze posture 78
frequencies, sound 38
funk styles of dance 87-88

G

gear 15
"Get Up, Get Into It, Get Involved" 40
glucose 32
golden era of hip-hop 81-82
Gooding, Cuba Jr. 80
graffiti artists 75
Grandmasters (DJs) 74
grasshoppers 98
grooves, isolation 40-43
Guess, the 65

H

Hall, Marcel Theo 56
Happy Feet 52-54
health information. *See* personal health information
hip-hop dance
  b-boyesque battle style 81-82
  benefits of studying 3
  choreography in movies 84
  commercialization of 84-86
  definition of 2
  forms of 87-100
  golden era of 81-82
  inspiration for 82
  Los Angeles style 83
  new style (nu style) 84
  origins 73-82
  social dances 79, 81
  as a subculture 73-74
  titles and descriptors for 82-84
  West Coast style 83
hip-hop freestyle 85
hip isolations 45
hippocampus 41*f*
hip pop isolation 45
hip roll isolation 45
Hit Dem Folks 71
house music 97-99
human backpack move 47
human beatboxers 74
Humpty Hump, the 64
hydration 33

I

injury
  prevention 27-29
  treatment 29-30
isolation grooves 40-43
isolations, described 8
isotonic muscle contraction 24-25, 25*f*

J

Jackson, Michael 94-95
Jersey Running Man, the 66
joint movements 26-27, 27*f*
joint stability 27
Juba, percussive style of 93

K

Kane, Big Daddy 97-98
Kid 'N Play Kickstep, the 60
kinesiology 25-27, 26*f*, 27*f*
kinesthetic awareness 4
kneepads 14

L

Latin Quarters 81
Lockers, The 90

locking 88-91
Los Angeles dance style 83
lung isolation 43-45

M

macronutrients 32
marley floors 20
Martin, Christopher "Play" 60
mental preparation 16
Milly Rock, the 70
MOP-TOP 95
movements
  across the floor 48
  combinations and sequences 10
  isolations 8
  joint movements 26-27, 27f
  moving across the floor 9-10
  pantomime 78
  polycentric 2, 8
  polyrhythms 2, 8
  rocking 8
muscular strength and endurance 17
muscular system 24-25, 24f
music
  as a guide to dance 3
  house music 97-99
  power of emotion in 37
  trans-Atlantic slave trade influence on 74
music awareness, using the body 37

N

Nation of Gods and Earths 75-76
neck isolations 42
neck strains 28
new style (nu style) dance style 84
nonfragmented rocking 48
nonverbal communication 3
nutrition 32-33

O

overload 31-32

P

pantomime movement 78
party rockin' 81
pecking 42
percussion, body 89
performance directions 49, 49f
personal health information 27
personal space 21-22
physical graffiti 75
physical preparation 17
polycentric movements 2, 8
polyrhythms 2, 8
popping 94-95
posers 91
posing 91
power of emotion in music 37

prefrontal cortex 41f
PRICED injury treatment 29-30
primary motor cortex 41f
Proctor, Tyrone 91-92
promptness 6-7
proteins 32-33
pulse 40
punking 91
PVC (polyvinyl chloride) floor covering 20

R

rappers (emcees) 3
Reid, Christopher "Kid" 60
rest 33
ring shout 75
Robot Shuffle 88
rocking 48, 77-78
rocking movement(s) 8
rock stepdrop bounce 4746
Rose, Tricia 85
Running Man, the 55

S

safety 20-22
Say What 42
Schloss, Joe 78
self-encouragement 16-17
sensory cortex 41f
sequences, movement combinations and 10
Sertima, Ivan Van 74
shin splints 29, 29f
shoes 14
shoulder isolations 42
single-hip roll isolation 45
Skate, the 58
skeletal system 22-24, 23f
skipping-rope-bounce 55
Smarth, Marjory "The Lotus" 97-99
Smith, Clarence Edward 75-76
social dances 79, 81
social phenomena of dance 73-74
Solomon, Sam "Boogaloo Sam" 93-95
Solomon, Timothy "Popping Pete" 94
Soul Brothers 96-97
Soul Train 89
sound frequencies 38
sounds, described 38
space 38
spatial awareness 21
Spongebob, the 67
sprung floors 20, 20f
stage directions 49, 49f
stance, alignment and 39, 39f
Steve Martin, the 59
strength and conditioning considerations 32
stretch reflex 18
students
  being present and prompt 6-7

students (*continued*)
  evaluation of class performance 7
  expectations and etiquette for 6-7
  preparing and practicing 6
  role of 5-6
studio safety 20-21
subchondral tissue 24
Supreme Mathematics 76
synovial joints 23, 26

T

teachers, role of 4-5
They Came Before Columbus (book) 74
time and tone 37-38, 37*k*
Tone Wop, the 69
torso isolations 43
Trac 2 77

U

Union Square 81

V

visual cortex 41*f*
visualization 16
vogue style of dance 91-92

W

waacking 91-92
Walk It Out 66
warm-up
  for flexibility 17
  for injury prevention 27-28, 39-40
  for moving across the floor 9
  purpose for 8, 30-31
  using line dances 52
West Coast dance style 83
Wild Style (movie) 79
Williams, Steve "Stezo" 59
writers (graffiti artists) 75
Wu-Tang, the 68